BLACKS AND WHITES

an experiment in racial indicators
Michael J. Flax

ISBN 87766-017-4
Library of Congress Catalog Card No. 72-165517
UI 85-136-5   1971

Available from:

Publications Office
The Urban Institute
2100 M Street, N.W.
Washington, D.C. 20037

List price: $1.50

Printed in the United States of America

Foreword

This report deals with the sensitive question of racial equality and attempts to present a balanced view of recent trends. The method of the report is to present indicator data for both blacks and whites over the period 1960 to 1968, relating to measurable social and economic matters. The data address such issues as:

—Comparisons of the levels of important indicators for blacks and whites in 1960 and 1968.
—Comparisons of the rates at which these indicators changed over the same period for both groups.
—Implications of both the levels and rates of change for equality and future change.

These indicators and explanations of them provide some reference points for improving the quality of the public and private interpretation, understanding and discussion of racial issues. Many have impressions about these issues; few have examined the range of data presented in this report to see what it shows.

Relatively few sets of racial indicators have been published. If the idea of racial indicators and other social indicators seems novel, it should be noted that indicators in the economic field, such as the gross national product (GNP) or consumer price index (CPI), are now widely accepted and widely used.

The report is directed primarily toward a general audience—government and business executives, civic leaders, journalists, and other concerned citizens. It is hoped, however, that it will be useful also to researchers and other specialists interested in the subject. An attempt has been made to present the material in a clear and understandable manner without sacrificing accuracy.

While many of the tables in this report present data for blacks and whites, in some cases only data for nonwhites and whites were available. As approximately 92 percent of nonwhites are blacks, the data on nonwhites reflect primarily a black population. The term "nonwhites" has been criticized, fairly in my judgment, as reflecting white ethnocentrism. The term nevertheless appears in this report to conform to common usage by those who gather and analyze data, including the Bureau of the Census and the Bureau of Labor Statistics. Its use here as a rough and approximate synonym for the black community should not be interpreted to mean that the Institute is unaware of or unconcerned with other minority groups.

Because an understanding of demography is crucial in interpreting racial data, Chapter 4 is devoted to the presentation of population trends. Blacks during the past ten years have become increasingly an urban population, highly concentrated in the larger central cities. This has important political, economic and social implications.

Many of the tables presented in this report are condensed and summarized and thus tend to conceal variations in the data. For instance, all tables in Chapter 1, and some others, are based on national data and thus do not indicate regional differences. Significant variations also are hidden by selecting certain age groups for examination, as in life expectancy; the 1969 data showed differing trends between these figures for blacks at age 35 and at age 25.

The preview chart on pages 10 and 11 summarizes all evaluation data included in the tables in Chapter 1 and provides the reader with an overview of the racial picture.

This report attempts to portray certain measurable inequalities between whites and nonwhites. The extremely complex questions of why these differences exist, and the still more difficult matter of deciding what to do about them, are not the province of this kind of factual report. What this report does do is provide the data necessary for knowing which questions should be asked and answered.

Because this work on racial indicators is an experimental approach and part of a long-term effort, suggestions or comments concerning the content or methodology of this report will be welcomed.

WILLIAM GORHAM
President
Washington, D. C.   The Urban Institute

Acknowledgments

The author wishes to make a general acknowledgment to all those whose individual work has provided relevant background information for such a report as this. This experiment in racial indicators would have been much more difficult had it not been for the theoretical and statistical research done in the field of measurement of racial differences during the past several years. The labors of the statistical agencies of the federal government, which provide data with a racial dimension, were also essential. In particular, the indicators presented in this work were derived from data published by the Bureau of the Census and the Bureau of Labor Statistics.

The initial impetus for this study was provided by several officials of the Ford Foundation who recognized the need for the development and dissemination of additional indicators in this important area of social concern.

In addition, many people contributed specifically to this paper: Martin V. Jones, Mitre Corporation, and J. Hollingworth, Emerson College, and the following Urban Institute personnel who provided advice with respect to the format and the content of this report: Peter B. Bloch, Joseph L. Caulfield, Pasqual A. DonVito, Harvey A. Garn, Harold W. Guthrie, Harry P. Hatry, William C. Leonard, Joseph H. Lewis, Walter Rybeck, Edward E. Wallace, and Clay H. Wellborn.

Harvey A. Garn, leader of the Indicators project, gave continuous assistance and support throughout the writing of this paper, and wrote Chapter 3. Jill Bury performed the mathematical computations and assisted Stuart Freeman with graphics. Mary Taylor provided major editorial help. Jacqueline Swingle assisted in the manuscript preparation.

Financial support was provided by the Department of Housing and Urban Development, and therefore the substance of this study is dedicated to the public. The author, however, takes full responsibility for the content of the report.

Contents

	Foreword	3
	Acknowledgments	5
Preview:	What the Racial Indicators of 1960–1968 Reveal	10
Chapter 1:	Racial Data: Three Perspectives	13
	1. Whites and Nonwhites Viewed Separately	15
	2. Comparing White and Nonwhite Progress	18
	3. Projecting 1960–1968 Trends	28
Chapter 2:	A Closer Look at Some Racial Comparisons	31
Chapter 3:	Income Distribution and Racial Equality	39
Chapter 4:	White and Black Population Trends	47
Appendix A:	A Tabulation of Indicators, with Formulas and Sample Calculations	61
Appendix B:	Methodology and Data Quality	78

Tables

1. Selected White/Nonwhite Data, 1960–1968 16
2. Rates of Change and Size of Gaps, 1960–1968 20
3. Differences in Rates of Change and Changes in Size of Gaps, 1960–1968 24
4. Projection of 1960–1968 Data Using Current Rates of Change 26
5. Approximate Year Nonwhite Levels Might Reach 1968 White Levels 29
6. Life Expectancy at Different Age Levels, 1960–1967 33
7. Percent of Occupied Substandard Housing (by Location), 1960–1968 34
8. Percent of Occupied Substandard Housing (by Region and Location), 1968 35
9. Median Years of School Completed by Persons 20 Years Old and Over (by Age), 1969 36
10. Median Income for White and Black Males 25–54 Years of Age (By Location and Years of School Completed), 1959–1967 37
11. Black Median Income as a Percent of White Median Income (by Location and Years of School Completed), 1959–1967 38
12. Occupational Distribution among Whites and Nonwhites and Unemployment Rates, 1960–1968 44
13. Median Earnings and Distribution by Occupation of Male Full-Time Employees in Central Cities, 1967–1968 45

TABLES

14. Effects of Occupational and Earning Disparities between Black and White Males, 1966–1967 46
15. Percent of the Total Black Population Living in Each Region of the United States, 1960–1969 49
16. Blacks as a Percent of the Total Population of the United States and of Each Region, 1960–1969 50
17. Percent of Population in Central Cities and Suburbs (by Region), 1960–1968 51
18. Blacks as a Percent of Total Population of Central Cities and Suburbs (by Region), 1960–1969 52
19. Percent of Blacks and Whites in Central Cities and Suburbs (by Size), 1960–1968 53
20. Percent of Blacks in the Total Population of Each of the Thirty Largest Cities, 1950–1967 54
21. Blacks as a Percent of the Total Population in Central Cities and Suburbs (by Size), 1960–1968 56
22. Percent of White and Black Population in the United States by Age and Sex, 1969 57
23. Percent of Population by Age in Central Cities, 1960–1968 58
24. Blacks as a Percent of Total Population in Central Cities by Age, 1960–1968 59
25. Summary Data Table 68
26. A Ranking Analysis of Selected Data 76

PREVIEW:
WHAT THE RACIAL INDICATORS OF 1960–1968 REVEAL

	IS THE DIRECTION OF CHANGE GENERALLY CONSIDERED DESIRABLE? Table 1 Whites and nonwhites considered separately		ARE NONWHITES CATCHING UP TO WHITES? Table 2 Comparison of white and nonwhite progress, 1960-1968	
Subject Characteristic	White	Nonwhite	Was the nonwhite rate of improvement greater than the white?	Was the size of the white/nonwhite gap decreasing?
LIVING CONDITIONS AND HEALTH				
Infant mortality (per 1,000 pop.)	YES	YES	NO	YES
Life expectancy at 35 years	YES	YES	YES	YES
HOUSING				
% Housing that is substandard	YES	YES	NO	YES
FAMILY				
% Female-headed families[a]	NO	NO	NO	NO
% Children living with two parents[a]	NO[b]	NO	NO	NO
Fertility rates (live births/1000 women, 15-54)[c]	YES	YES	NO	YES
% Illegitimate births[d]	NO	NO	YES[e]	NO
EDUCATION				
% Men (age 25-29) completing high school	YES	YES	YES	YES
% Completing at least 4 yrs. of college (25-34)	YES	YES	YES	NO
EMPLOYMENT				
% Unemployed	YES	YES	NO	YES
% Teenagers unemployed	YES	YES	NO	YES
% In clerical occupations	YES	YES	YES	YES
% In professional and technical occupations	YES	YES	YES	YES
INCOME AND POVERTY				
Median family income (in 1968 dollars)	YES	YES	YES	NO
% Persons below poverty level	YES	YES	NO	YES
% Families with incomes greater than $8,000	YES	YES	YES	NO

a. A rise in the proportion of children living with two parents or a decline in the proportion of female-headed families is generally thought to indicate a tendency toward greater family stability. This does not deny that similar figures for these variables may have different implications for the white and nonwhite communities because of cultural differences.

b. Data indicate that no change occurred.

c. A lowering of the fertility rate is assumed desirable. Where income is limited a decrease would tend to encourage desirable

10

WHITE/NONWHITE DIFFERENCES IF RECENT RATES OF CHANGE CONTINUE
Table 3
Assuming the 1960-1968 rates of change remain the same...

FUTURE POSSIBILITIES
Table 4
Assuming the 1960-1968 nonwhite rates of change remain the same...

Would the size of the white/nonwhite gap be smaller in 1976 than 1968?	Would nonwhites ever reach 1968 white levels?	Rank[f]	Approximate year when nonwhite levels might reach 1968 white levels
YES	YES	12	1994
YES	YES	13	2019
YES	YES	9	1988
NO	NO	15	never
NO	NO	16	never
YES	YES	6	1979
NO	NO	14	never
YES	YES	1	1973
NO	YES	8	1987
YES	YES	7	1982
YES	YES	10	1989
YES	YES	2	1974
YES	YES	4	1978
NO	YES	5	1978
YES	YES	11	1992
YES	YES	3	1974

trends in many of the other categories measured.

d. Attitudes toward illegitimacy affecting accuracy of reporting have been found to differ among whites and nonwhites, therefore, the significance of similar figures may not be the same. It is assumed here that a higher illegitimacy rate is not desirable.

e. The white illegitimacy rate is increasing at double the nonwhite rate, therefore the slower nonwhite change may be expressed as a relatively greater "rate of improvement."

f. The earliest year is ranked lowest (1).

11

Chapter 1

Racial Data: Three Perspectives

This chapter presents in a straightforward manner data on many aspects of white and nonwhite[1] socio-economic differences. Three main objectives are stressed in presenting the data:

    1. Providing a rough guide to the magnitude of differences in selected socio-economic areas.

    2. Showing whether the rate of change is favorable or unfavorable from the standpoint of equality.

    3. Emphasizing how data sometimes can legitimately indicate several conflicting trends.

The third objective is particularly important in that the progress of nonwhites can be made to look good or poor depending upon how the data are used. Some of the confusion which exists today regarding the progress of nonwhites is probably due to presenting data from only one perspective. For example, if a man earning $16,000 a year gets a 5 percent raise and another earning $10,000 a year gets a 7 percent raise, it is true that the second obtains a larger relative or percentage raise. On the other hand, it is also true that the first receives a larger absolute raise ($800 vs. $700). The difference between the two salaries increases from $6,000 before the raise to $6,100 afterwards. Different conclusions can be drawn depending upon whether the

    1. Wherever possible data for whites and blacks are used, but in many cases only data for nonwhites (about 92 percent are black) and whites were available. The term nonwhite is used where data for blacks are not classified separately. For a representative recent bibliography relating to racial differences, see: Albert Wohlstetter and Sinclair Coleman, *Race Differences in Income* (Santa Monica, Calif.: The Rand Corporation, 1970), pp. 105-109.

focus is on the percentage raise, on the difference of actual income, or—as it should be—on both sets of data. This explains one way in which seemingly contradictory interpretations regarding the nonwhite progress may emerge from the same statistics.

This chapter is divided into three parts, beginning with the more simple and proceeding to the more complex.

The first part looks at the whites and the nonwhites separately and measures whether, in selected social and economic matters, the two racial groups have progressed between 1960 and 1968.

The second part, in contrast to the first, compares the progress of nonwhites with that of whites and illustrates how this comparison may lead to alternative interpretations of data. As shown in the example given earlier, different evaluations can result from contrasting white and nonwhite rates of change with the change in the absolute differences between whites and nonwhites between 1960 and 1968. The difference between whites and nonwhites at a given point of time is called the white/nonwhite gap.

The third part examines future chances for racial equality assuming that the same recent rates of change continue in coming years.

The socio-economic characteristics chosen are selective, not exhaustive. Two considerations in choosing them were that data were available for the past decade, and that the federal government collects these data frequently, permitting the indicators to be regularly updated.

1. WHITES AND NONWHITES VIEWED SEPARATELY

The righthand column of Table 1 poses the question:

> *Between the years 1960 and 1968 has the direction of change in certain important aspects of life been generally favorable for whites and nonwhites?*

While some people do hold different views concerning what is favorable and unfavorable, there is for each aspect or indicator a wide consensus regarding the desired direction of change, and this common view of what constitutes progress is followed here. Most controversial are what constitute favorable family characteristics, and especially fertility rates.

There are, of course, many other possible indices—congestion, air pollution, alienation, morale, to name but a few—which should be included in evaluating whether the quality of life has improved or worsened for all people, regardless of race. The indicators included here are those which are commonly used in measuring racial differences and, therefore, are those for which data were available. Furthermore, this report is an experiment in the use of racial indicators; future studies may include additional indices so a more comprehensive evaluation of the quality of life can be given.

In this table each racial group is compared to its own past record. The changes for both whites and nonwhites appear undesirable in terms of certain family indicators, namely, children living with two parents, female-headed families, and illegitimacy. According to all other measures, whites and nonwhites have experienced generally desirable directions of change.

Table 1 also includes the basic data used for the 1960-1968 comparisons. Providing data for only two different years permits the presentation of a large number of characteristics in a clear and consistent manner. The reader can spot where differences in the comparisons are small or large and appear important or unimportant. For instance, the decline in infant mortality was far less than the decline of those living in housing that is substandard. Yet the use of two data points—as contrasted with a series of data for all intervening years—presents difficulties. The primary one is that this method does not reveal certain important features of change, for instance, whether a particularly big shift took place close to 1960 and then lost its momentum, whether it reflects a more recent trend that is gaining momentum, or whether the changes have been too erratic to constitute a trend.[2]

---

2. This and other methodological difficulties are discussed further in Appendix B.

Table 1. **SELECTED WHITE/NONWHITE DATA: 1960–1968**

W — White; NW — Nonwhite; B — Black. About 92% of nonwhites are black.[a]

		DATA		EVALUATION
INDICATORS		1960	1968	Is the direction of change generally considered desirable?
LIVING CONDITIONS AND HEALTH				
Infant mortality (per 1000 population)[b]	W	17.2	14.7[c]	yes
	NW	26.9	23.4[c]	yes
Life expectancy at 35 years[d]	W	73.8yrs.	74.4yrs.[c]	yes
	NW	69.3yrs.	70.0yrs.[c]	yes
HOUSING				
% Housing that is substandard	W	13%	6%	yes
	NW	44%	24%	yes
FAMILY				
% Female-headed families[e]	W	8.7%	8.9%	no
	NW	22.4%	26.4%	no
% Children living with two parents[e]	W	92%	92%	no[f]
	NW	75%	69%	no
Fertility rates (live births/1000 women age 15-44)	W	113	79.4[c]	yes[g]
	NW	154	115.8[c]	yes
% Illegitimate births	W	2.3%	5.5%[c]	no[h]
	NW	21.6%	30.7%[c]	no
EDUCATION				
% Men (age 25-29) completing high school	W	63%	76%	yes
	B	36%[i]	58%	yes

Source of Data: *The Social and Economic Status of Negroes in the United States, 1969,* BLS Report No. 375, Current Population Reports, Series P-23, No. 29, Bureaus of the Census and of Labor Statistics (Washington, D.C.: U.S. Government Printing Office, 1970).

a. Black data are used whenever available.

b. Infants dying at less than one month of age.

c. 1968 values were extrapolated from 1960-1967 or 1960-1969 rates of change.

d. Data on life expectancy look more favorable as the age group rises. (See Table 6.)

e. A rise in the proportion of children living with two parents and a decline in the proportion of female-headed families is generally thought to indicate a tendency toward greater family stability. This does not deny that similar firgures for these variables may have different implications for

		DATA		EVALUATION
INDICATORS—continued		1960	1968	Is the direction of change generally considered desirable?

EDUCATION—continued

% Completing at least four years college (25–34 yrs.)	W	11.7%	15.7%c	yes
	B	4.3%	6.3%c	yes

EMPLOYMENT

% Unemployed	W	4.9%	3.2%	yes
	NW	10.2%	6.7%	yes
% Teenagers Unemployed	W	19.1%	11%	yes
	NW	34.2%	25%	yes
% In clerical occupations	W	15.8%	17.5%c	yes
	NW	7.3%	12.1%c	yes
% In professional and technical occupations	W	12.1%	14.2%c	yes
	NW	4.8%	7.8%c	yes

INCOME AND POVERTY

Median family income (in 1968 dollars)	W	$6857	$8937	yes
	NW	$3794	$5590	yes
% Persons below poverty level[j]	W	18%	10%	yes
	B	55%	35%	yes
% Families with incomes greater than $8,000 (in 1968 dollars)	W	39%	58%	yes
	NW	15%	32%	yes

the white and nonwhite communities because of cultural differences.

f. Data indicate that no change has occurred.

g. A lowering of the fertility rate is assumed to be desirable. Where income is limited a decrease would tend to encourage desirable trends in many of the other categories measured.

h. Attitudes toward illegitimacy affecting accuracy of reporting have been found to differ among whites and nonwhites, therefore the significance of similar figures may not be the same. It is assumed here that a higher illegitimacy rate is not desirable.

i. Nonwhite data are used for 1960.

j. The poverty level is different for farm and nonfarm families and depends on national cost of living and size of family. In 1968 the nonfarm family of 4 poverty level was $3553.

2. COMPARING WHITE AND NONWHITE PROGRESS

Having looked at data to measure the progress of whites and nonwhites separately, the focus of attention is now shifted to compare the progress of whites and nonwhites between 1960 and 1968. As was shown in the example on page 13, alternative interpretations can be made about the progress toward equality when both rates of change and gaps are presented together.

Table 2 poses the frequently asked question:

Are nonwhites catching up to whites?

Two criteria for evaluating progress are used:

1. *Was the rate of nonwhite improvement greater than that for the whites in the 1960-1968 period?*

2. *Was the size of the white/nonwhite gap decreasing in the 1960-1968 period?*

For two of the sixteen indicators, the answer to both questions is no. For four of the indicators, the answer to both questions is yes. But for most of the indicators, ten of them, the answer is yes and no.

Thus it is apparent that one can describe the progress of nonwhites in these respects as either good or poor. However, a more accurate picture is given by presenting both sets of data together.

A further look at Table 2 shows that for half of the indicators used, the whites showed improvement at a greater rate than the nonwhites, and vice versa for the other half. On the other hand, the size of the gap between whites and nonwhites was narrowed in ten of the measures, but increased in the other six.

Table 2 also expresses the data quantitatively. Using, for example, the median family income figures (first in the set of Income and Poverty indicators), the reader will note that columns 1 and 2 contain the same data as given in Table 1. Column 3, by using the compound interest formula,[3] shows the annual rate of change that would have been necessary to arrive at the changes in value between the 1960 and 1968 data. For example, in order for the average salaries of whites, $6,857 in 1960, to increase to $8,937 in 1968 the average salary increases per annum would have had to be 3.4 percent. This figure is labeled "imputed annual rate of change" because the two data points (1960 and 1968) do not establish that there was a constant rate of change over the period. A constant rate of change is postulated only for clarity and as a basis for comparisons. The black downward pointing arrow next to the percentage figure indicates that the rate of change has tended to decrease white/nonwhite differences. That is, the rate of change was greater and more favorable for the nonwhites (4.9 percent vs. 3.4 percent). Columns

---

3. See Appendix A for a discussion of these calculations and related issues.

4 and 5 state the size of the white/nonwhite gap in 1960 and 1968 respectively.[4] This gap is calculated by taking the difference between the white and nonwhite values for each of the two years ($6,857 − $3,794 = $3,063). The red upward pointing arrow next to the figure in Column 5 indicates that the size of the gap increased from 1960 to 1968 ($3,063 to $3,347).

As has been shown, median family income illustrates how alternative interpretations are permissible. Despite nonwhite gains with regard to rates of change (the nonwhite rate of change is greater—4.9 percent compared to 3.4 percent), the actual dollar gap widened from 1960 to 1968 ($3,063 to $3,347). This phenomenon of rates of change favoring the nonwhites, but accompanied by an increasing size of the white/nonwhite gap, occurs in the following variables:

> % Illegitimate births
> % Completing at least 4 years of college
> Median family income
> % Families with incomes greater than $8,000 (in 1968 dollars)

Conversely, infant mortality is a case in which whites experienced greater favorable rates of change but yet the white/nonwhite gap decreased between 1960 and 1968. Indicators where this phenomenon occurs include:

> Infant mortality   % Unemployed
> % Housing that is substandard   % Teenagers unemployed
> Fertility rates   % Persons below poverty level

Table 3 shows in still another way the divergence between the rate of change relationships and the change in the size of the gap. Column 4 gives the difference in rates of change by subtracting the rates of change for whites and nonwhites (Column 3).

For example, in the case of median family income the difference in rates of changes is 1.5 percent (4.9 percent − 3.4 percent). Column 5 shows the percent change in the size of the white/nonwhite gap between 1960 and 1968. The numbers next to the percentage figures in columns 4 and 5 show how median income ranks with other indicators with respect to rates of change and change in the gap size. A rank of 1 is best and of 16 is worst in terms of progress toward equality.

4. It should be noted that where figures in columns 1 and 2 are given in percentages, the rate of change has been calculated between two percentage figures. For example, the percent of white persons below the poverty level decreased from 18 percent to 10 percent between 1960 and 1968. This was equivalent to an annual 7.1 percent decrease in the percentage figure. It should not be construed as an annual 7.1 percent decrease in the *number* of whites below the poverty level. Similarly, many of the gaps are differences in percentages obtained by subtraction. In the case of unemployment, infant mortality, and crime rates, for example, rates and magnitudes of change are commonly calculated in this manner.

Table 2. RATES OF CHANGE AND SIZE OF GAPS: 1960–1968*

W — White; NW — Nonwhite; B — Black. About 92% of nonwhites are black.[a]

Rates tend to: △ increase difference   Size of gap: ▲ increasing
  ▽ decrease difference   ▼ decreasing

INDICATOR		DATA 1960	DATA 1968	Imputed annual rate of change 1960-1968[b]	
LIVING CONDITIONS AND HEALTH					
Infant mortality (per 1000 population)[d]	W	17.2	14.7[e]	−2.0%	△
	NW	26.9	23.4[e]	−1.8%	
Life expectancy at 35 years[f]	W	73.8 yrs.	74.4 yrs.[e]	+0.10%	▽
	NW	69.3 yrs.	70.0 yrs.[e]	+0.12%	
HOUSING					
% Housing that is substandard	W	13%	6%	−9.2%	△
	NW	44%	24%	−7.3%	
FAMILY					
% Female-headed families	W	8.7%	8.9%	+ 0.3%	△
	NW	22.4%	26.4%	+ 2.1%	
% Children living with two parents	W	92%	92%	0.0	△
	NW	75%	69%	−1.1%	
Fertility rates (live birth/1000 women, age 15-44 years)[g]	W	113	79.4[e]	−4.3%	△
	NW	154	115.8[e]	−3.5%	
% Illegitimate births[h]	W	2.3%	5.5%[e]	+ 11.4%	▽
	NW	21.6%	30.7%[e]	+ 4.5%	
EDUCATION					
% Men (age 25-29) completing high school	W	63%	76%	+ 2.3%	▽
	B	36%[i]	58%	+ 6.1%	
% Completing at least 4 years of college (25-34 years)	W	11.7%	15.7%	+ 3.8%	▽
	B	4.3%	6.3%	+ 4.9%	

ANALYSIS			EVALUATION	
Size of white/nonwhite gap, 1960c	Size of white/nonwhite gap, 1968c		Was the nonwhite rate of improvement greater than the white?	Was the size of the white/nonwhite gap decreasing?
9.7%	8.7%	▼	no	yes
4.5 yrs.	4.4 yrs.	▼	yes	yes
31%	18%	▼	no	yes
13.7%	17.5%	▲	no [k]	no
17%	23%	▲	no [l]	no
41%	36.4%	▼	no	yes
19.3%	25.2%	▲	yes [m]	no
27%	18%	▼	yes	yes
7.4%	9.0%	▲	yes	no

* Footnotes are at the end of the table, on pages 22–23.

Table 2. **RATES OF CHANGE AND SIZE OF GAPS: 1960–1968** —CONTINUED

W — White; NW — Nonwhite; B — Black. About 92% of nonwhites are black.[a]

Rates tend to: △ increase difference   Size of gap: ▲ increasing
              ▽ decrease difference   ▼ decreasing

INDICATOR		DATA 1960	DATA 1968	Imputed annual rate of change 1960-1968[b]	
EMPLOYMENT					
% Unemployed	W	4.9%	3.2%	−5.2%	△
	NW	10.2%	6.7%	−5.1%	
% Teenagers unemployed	W	19.1%	11%	−6.7%	△
	NW	34.2%	25%	−3.9%	
% In clerical occupations	W	15.8%	17.5%[e]	+1.3%	▽
	NW	7.3%	12.1%[e]	+6.6%	
% In professional and technical occupations	W	12.1%	14.2%[e]	+2.0%	▽
	NW	4.8%	7.8%[e]	+6.2%	
INCOME AND POVERTY					
Median family income (in 1968 dollars)	W	$6857	$8937	+3.4%	▽
	NW	$3794	$5590	+4.9%	
% Persons below poverty level[j]	W	18%	10%	−7.1%	△
	B	55%	35%	−5.5%	
% Families with incomes greater than $8000 (in 1968 dollars)	W	39%	58%	+4.8%	▽
	NW	15%	32%	+10.0%	

Source of Data: *The Social and Economic Status of the Negroes in the United States, 1969.*

a. Black data are used whenever available.
b. This is the annual percentage increase that would give the 1960-1968 change if compounded annually from 1960-1968. Many of these figures are percentage increases in percentages.
c. Many of these gaps are differences between white and nonwhite percentage figures.
d. Infants dying at less than one month of age.
e. 1968 values were extrapolated from 1960-1967 or 1960-1969 rates of change.
f. Data on life expectancy look more favorable as the age group rises. (See Table 6.)
g. A lowering of the fertility rate is assumed desirable. Where income is limited a de-

ANALYSIS			EVALUATION	
Size of white/nonwhite gap, 1960[c]	Size of white/nonwhite gap, 1968[c]		Was the nonwhite rate of improvement greater than the white?	Was the size of the white/nonwhite gap decreasing?
5.3%	3.5%	▼	no	yes
15.1%	14%	▼	no	yes
8.5%	5.4%	▼	yes	yes
7.3%	6.4%	▼	yes	yes
$3063	$3347	▲	yes	no
37%	25%	▼	no	yes
24%	26%	▲	yes	no

crease would tend to encourage desirable trends in many of the other categories measured.

h. The white illegitimacy rate is increasing at double the nonwhite rate, therefore the slower nonwhite change may be expressed as a relatively greater "rate of improvement."

i. 1960 data are for nonwhites.

j. See footnote j of Table 1, page 17.

k. The number of female-headed families is increasing for both whites and nonwhites, but the number of female-headed nonwhite families is increasing at a faster rate.

l. The percent of nonwhite children living with two parents is decreasing, while the percent of white children remains the same.

m. The percent of both white and nonwhite illegitimate births is increasing, but that of whites is increasing at a faster rate.

Table 3. **DIFFERENCES IN RATES OF CHANGE AND CHANGES IN SIZE OF GAPS: 1960–1968**

W—White; NW—Nonwhite; B—Black. About 92% of nonwhites are black.[a]

Rates tend to: △ increase differences
△▽ decrease differences

Size of gap: ▲ increasing
▼ decreasing

			DATA		ANALYSIS			
INDICATORS		1960	1968	Imputed annual rate of change 1960-1968[b]	Difference in rates of change: 1960-68	Rank[c]	Percent change in white/nonwhite gap size 1960-68	Rank[c]
LIVING CONDITIONS AND HEALTH								
Infant mortality (per 1000 population)	W	17.2	14.7[f]	−2.0%	−0.2% △	(10)	−11% ▼	(7-8)
	NW	26.9	23.4[f]	−1.8%				
Life expectancy at 35 years[e]	W	73.8yrs.	74.4yrs.[f]	+0.10%	+.02% ▽	(8)	−2.2% ▼	(11)
	NW	69.3yrs.	70.0yrs.[f]	+0.12%				
HOUSING								
% Housing that is substandard	W	13%	6%	−9.2%	−1.9% △	(15)	−42% ▼	(1)
	NW	44%	24%	−7.3%				
FAMILY								
% Female-headed families	W	8.7%	8.9%	+0.3%	−1.8% △	(14)	+28% ▲	(14)
	NW	22.4%	26.4%	+2.1%				
% Children living with two parents	W	92%	92%	0.0	−1.1% △	(12)	+35% ▲	(16)
	NW	75%	69%	−1.1%				
Fertility rates (live births/ 1000 women, 15-44)	W	113	79.4[f]	−4.3%	−0.8% △	(11)	−11% ▼	(7-8)
	NW	154	115.8[f]	−3.5%				
% Illegitimate births	W	2.3%	5.5%[f]	+11.4%	+6.9% ▽	(1)	+31% ▲	(15)
	NW	21.6%	30.7%[f]	+ 4.5%				
EDUCATION								
% Men (age 25-29) completing high school	W	63%	76%	+2.3%	+3.8% ▽	(5)	−33% ▼	(4)
	B	36%[h]	58%	+6.1%				

Source of Data: *The Social and Economic Status of Negroes in the United States, 1969.*

a. Black data are used whenever available.
b. This is the annual percentage increase that would give the 1960-1968 change if compounded annually from 1969-1968. Many of these figures are percentage increases in percentages.

		DATA			ANALYSIS			
INDICATORS—continued		1960	1968	Imputed annual rate of change 1960-1968[b]	Difference in rates of change: 1960-68	Rank[c]	Percent change in white/nonwhite gap size 1960-68	Rank[c]

EDUCATION—continued

| % Completing at least 4 yrs. of college (25-34) | W | 11.7% | 15.7% | +3.8% | +1.1% ▽ | (7) | +21% ▲ | (13) |
| | B | 4.3% | 6.3% | +4.9% | | | | |

EMPLOYMENT

% Unemployed	W	4.9%	3.2%	−5.2%	−0.1% △	(9)	−34% ▼	(3)
	NW	10.2%	6.7%	−5.1%				
% Teenagers unemployed	W	19.1%	11%	−6.7%	−2.8% △	(16)	−7.5% ▼	(10)
	NW	34.2%	25%	−3.9%				
% In clerical occupations	W	15.8%	17.5%[f]	+1.3%	+5.3% ▽	(2)	−37% ▼	(2)
	NW	7.3%	12.1%[f]	+6.6%				
% In professional and technical occupations	W	12.1%	14.2%[f]	+2.0%	+4.3% ▽	(4)	−13% ▼	(6)
	NW	4.8%	7.8%[f]	+6.2%				

INCOME AND POVERTY

Median family income (in 1968 dollars)	W	$6857	$8937	+3.4%	+1.5% ▽	(6)	+9.3% ▲	(12)
	NW	$3794	$5590	+4.9%				
% Persons below poverty level	W	18%	10%	−7.1%	−1.6% △	(13)	−32% ▼	(5)
	B	55%	35%	−5.5%				
% Families with incomes greater than $8,000	W	39%	58%	+4.8%	+5.2% ▽	(3)	+8.3% ▲	(9)
	NW	15%	32%	+10.0%				

c. A rank of 1 indicates the greatest improvement toward equality.

d. Infants dying at less than one month of age.

e. Data on life expectancy look more favorable as the age group rises. (See Table 6.)

f. 1968 values were computed from 1960-1967 or 1960-1969 rates of change.

g. 1960 data are for nonwhites.

h. Nonwhite data is used for 1960.

Table 4. PROJECTION OF 1960-1968 DATA USING CURRENT RATES OF CHANGE

Size of gap: + larger in 1976, − smaller in 1976

INDICATORS	ANALYSIS — Estimated percent change in white/nonwhite gap size: 1968-76[a]	Rank[b]	Approximate year nonwhite levels might reach 1968 white levels: Year	Rank[b]	EVALUATION — Would the size of the white/nonwhite gap be smaller in 1976 than it was in 1968?	Would nonwhites ever reach 1968 white levels?
LIVING CONDITIONS AND HEALTH						
Infant mortality (per 1,000 population)[c]	−11%	(10)	1994	(12)	yes	yes
Life expectancy at 35 years[d]	− 3%	(11)	2019	(13)	yes	yes
HOUSING						
% Housing that is substandard	−43%	(3)	1988	(9)	yes	yes
FAMILY						
% Female-headed families	+26%	(15)	never	(15)	no	no
% Children living with two parents	+24%	(14)	never	(16)	no	no
Fertility rates	−14%	(9)	1979	(6)	yes	yes
% Illegitimate births	+21%	(13)	never	(14)	no	no
EDUCATION						
% Men (age 25-29) completing high school	−110%[e]	(2)	1973	(1)	yes	yes

Source of Data: *The Social and Economic Status of Negroes in the United States, 1969.*

a. 1976 was chosen because it represents an eight-year period (1968-1976) as does 1960-1968.

| | ANALYSIS || EVALUATION ||
INDICATORS—continued	Estimated percent change in white/ nonwhite gap size: 1968-76[a]	Rank[b]	Approximate year nonwhite levels might reach 1968 white levels: Year	Rank[b]	Would the size of the white/ nonwhite gap be smaller in 1976 than it was in 1968?	Would nonwhites ever reach 1968 white levels?
EDUCATION—continued						
% Completing at least 4 years of college (25-34 yrs)	+34%	(16)	1987	(8)	no	yes
EMPLOYMENT						
% Unemployed	−34%	(5)	1982	(7)	yes	yes
% Teenagers unemployed	−15%	(8)	1989	(10)	yes	yes
% In clerical occupations	−114%[e]	(1)	1974	(2)	yes	yes
% In professional occupations	−40%	(4)	1978	(5)	yes	yes
INCOME AND POVERTY						
Median family income	+2%	(12)	1978	(4)	no	yes
% Persons below poverty level	−33%	(6)	1992	(11)	yes	yes
% Families with income greater than $8,000 (1968$)	−30%	(7)	1974	(3)	yes	yes

b. A rank of 1 indicates the greatest nonwhite improvement.
c. Infants dying at less than one month of age.
d. Data on life expectancy look more favorable as the age group rises. (See Table 6.)
e. If present rates of change should remain the same, the gap will have closed before 1976 and the whites would have the lower values.

3. PROJECTING 1960-1968 TRENDS

Another way of understanding the implications of the 1960-1968 data is shown in Table 4. Columns 3 and 4 examine the data by projecting recent experience in two ways:

> 1. *Assuming that the 1960-1968 rates of change stay the same,*[5] *would the size of the white/nonwhite gap be smaller in 1976*[6] *than it was in 1968?*
>
> 2. *If the nonwhite rate of change stays at its recent rate, would nonwhites ever reach the level whites had already attained by 1968?*

The answers reflect *projections* of past data, *not predictions* of what the future necessarily holds.

Even a brief consideration of the large number of possible interaction and feedback effects among the sixteen variables examined here suggests the dangers of attempting to predict the future by simply extrapolating past data. For example, one cannot ignore the effects of education on median income and vice versa.[7] Social and technological modifications occurring in society must also be taken into account. Furthermore, some variables (such as unemployment rates) have known cyclical variations. Simple extrapolation does not take such variations into account.

Possible effects of a continuation of the 1960-1968 rates of change on the sixteen socio-economic variables examined are summarized in columns 1 and 2 and evaluated in columns 3 and 4 of Table 4.

Table 5 gives in ranking order the approximate year when nonwhite levels might reach 1968 white levels.

---

5. Actually, the rates of change are not likely to remain at the same level. As the nonwhite levels approach those of the whites, the rates of change of the nonwhites can be expected to approximate more nearly that of the whites. See Harvey A. Garn, "Nonwhite Gains—Present Policy Trends," U.I. Paper 113-23 (Washington, D.C.: The Urban Institute, 1969).

6. The year of the national centennial, 1976, was picked because it represents an eight-year period (1968-1976) as does 1960-1968.

7. This and related matters are discussed further in Chapter 3.

Table 5.

APPROXIMATE YEAR NONWHITE LEVELS MIGHT REACH 1968 WHITE LEVELS[a]

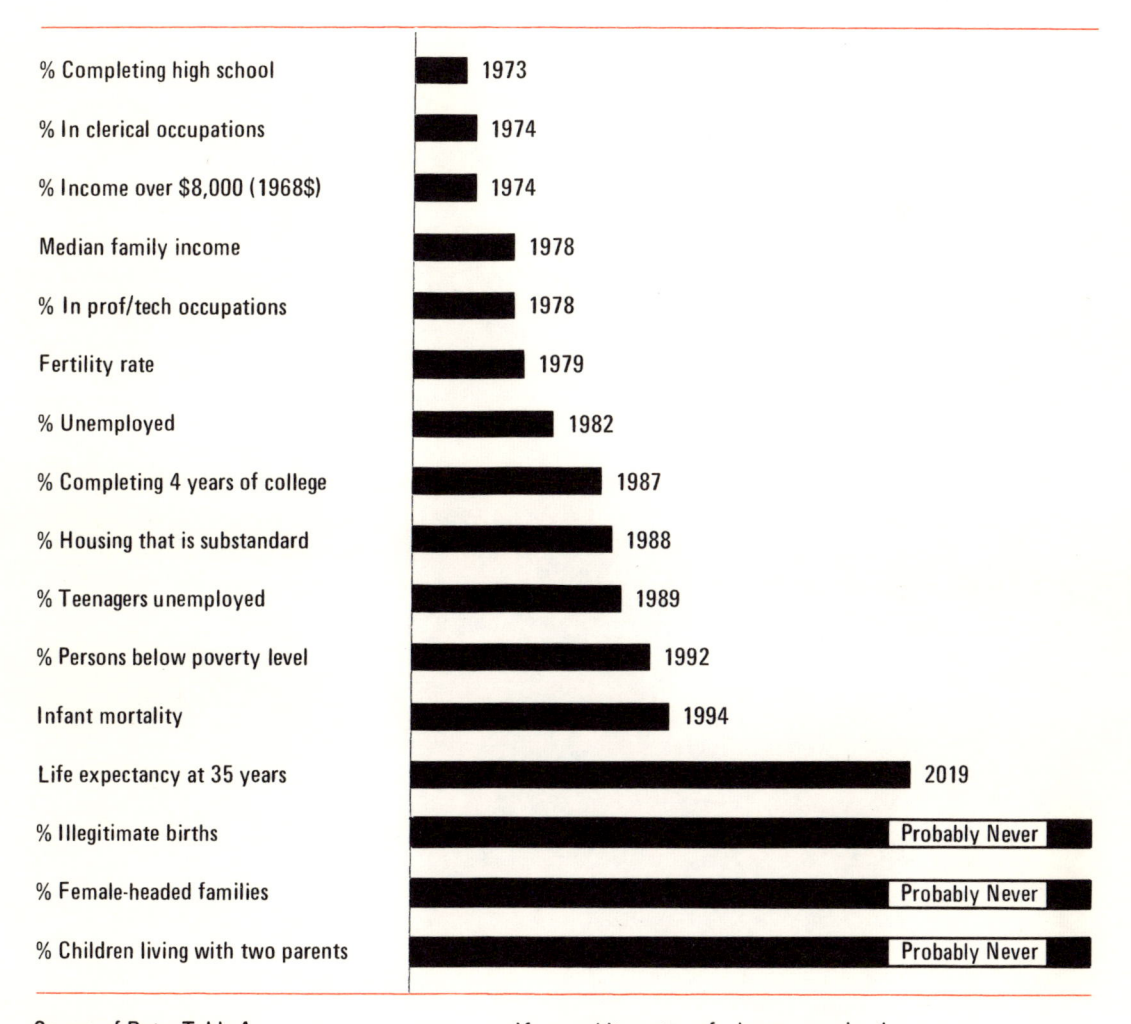

% Completing high school	1973
% In clerical occupations	1974
% Income over $8,000 (1968$)	1974
Median family income	1978
% In prof/tech occupations	1978
Fertility rate	1979
% Unemployed	1982
% Completing 4 years of college	1987
% Housing that is substandard	1988
% Teenagers unemployed	1989
% Persons below poverty level	1992
Infant mortality	1994
Life expectancy at 35 years	2019
% Illegitimate births	Probably Never
% Female-headed families	Probably Never
% Children living with two parents	Probably Never

Source of Data: Table 4.

a. If nonwhite rates of change remain the same as they were during 1960-1968.

Chapter 2

A Closer Look at Some Racial Comparisons

This chapter presents a more detailed set of data on four indicators—life expectancy, housing, education, and median income—and shows how particular categories within each indicator can portray a different picture from the whole. While the tables included here are meant to be largely self-explanatory, some of the findings are worthy of discussion[1]:

Life Expectancy: Table 6 shows that variations in rates of change and gap size between whites and nonwhites are small for all age groups, but that the gaps are closing very little if at all. In fact, the white/nonwhite gap widened for the 25-year-old group. The life expectancy figures at age 35 were used in the tables in Chapter 1; had the figures for the 25-year-old group been used, a more pessimistic picture would have emerged.

Housing: Table 7 demonstrates that the rates of change and the gap closure for those living in substandard housing have been relatively favorable for whites and nonwhites. Note, however, that the change was least favorable for nonwhites living in nonmetropolitan areas.[2] The figures for the United States as a whole were used in the tables in Chapter 1 and, as can be seen in Table 8, there are considerable regional variations. The condition of nonwhite housing in the South is much worse than it is in all the rest of the United States.

---

1. Note that other points of time (e.g., 1960-1967) are used where data are more complete than for 1960-1968.
2. Metropolitan areas, which include about two-thirds of the United States population, consist of cities with a population over 50,000 and their associated suburban counties. Nonmetropolitan areas consist of the remainder of the United States, including rural areas.

Education: Table 9 looks at the median school years completed by persons of different age groups and by race. Assuming that one completes high school by age 20 at the very latest, note that both whites and blacks experienced dramatic improvement each decade until the 1940's. (The 45-54-year-old group would have completed high school around 1943.) Most whites in the 45-54-year-old group have completed high school, whereas the blacks do not reach that level until the 30-34-year-old group who finished high school about 1959. In other words, the whites completed their big educational advance in the early 1940's and the blacks completed theirs in the late 1950's. Since 1959 (those younger than the 30-34 age groups) both whites and blacks have been advancing at approximately the same rate, hence the abrupt decrease in the gap and its leveling off.

Median Income: The tabulation in Table 10 of median income in relation to years of school completed shows that the black rate of income growth is larger and the gap size is generally decreasing. This apparent contradiction with Table 2, which reveals that the gap size is increasing, can be accounted for by several factors. First, Table 2 looks at family income while Table 10 refers only to income of males; second, Table 2 includes all age groups and Table 10 is confined to the 25-54-year bracket; third, Table 2 data are based on all nonwhites in the nation and Table 10 data are taken only from blacks living in metropolitan areas. These two tables are a vivid illustration of how the picture for selected groups can be quite different from national averages.

An exception in Table 10 to the decrease in gap size is among suburban blacks who have partially completed high school. Compared with whites in the same location and with the same amount of schooling, the size of the gap is substantially widening. Not surprisingly, the variation in black median income for different educational levels, as exhibited in Table 11, follows roughly the same pattern.

Table 6.

LIFE EXPECTANCY AT DIFFERENT AGE LEVELS: 1960–1967

	DATA			EVALUATION[a]	
AGE LEVEL	1960	1967	Imputed annual rate of change 1960-1967[b]	White/non-white gap 1967 (in years)	Percent change in gap size 1960-1967
	(in years)				
25 years					
W	73.3	73.8	+0.09%	−5.3	+1.9%
NW	68.1	68.5	+0.08%		
35 years					
W	73.8	74.3	+0.10%	−4.4	−2.2%
NW	69.3	69.9	+0.12%		
45 years					
W	74.7	75.2	+0.16%	−3.3	−5.7%
NW	71.2	71.9	+0.14%		
55 years					
W	76.5	77.0	+0.09%	−2.1	−4.5%
NW	74.3	74.9	+0.12%		

Source of Data: *The Social and Economic Status of Negroes in the United States, 1969,* p. 64.

a. A plus sign means a widening of the gap and a worsening situation from the standpoint of equality, while a minus sign means a diminishing of the gap.

b. Imputed annual compound interest rate needed during 1960 to 1967 in order to account for the recorded change.

Table 7

PERCENT OF OCCUPIED SUBSTANDARD HOUSING (BY LOCATION), 1960–1968

	\multicolumn{3}{c}{DATA}	\multicolumn{2}{c}{EVALUATION}
LOCATION	Percent in 1960	1968	Imputed annual rate of change[a]	Size of white/non-white gap 1968[b]	Percent reduction in size of white/nonwhite gap, 1960-1968
United States					
W	13%	6%	−9.2%	18%	−42%
NW	44%	24%	−7.3%		
Central cities					
W	8%	3%	−11.5%	6%	−65%
NW	25%	9%	−12.0%		
Suburbs					
W	7%	3%	−10.0%	13%	−64%
NW	43%	16%	−11.4%		
Nonmetropolitan areas					
W	23%	11%	−9.0%	44%	−19%
NW	77%	55%	−4.1%		

Source of Data: *Social and Economic Status of Negroes in the United States, 1969,* p. 57.

a. This is the annual compound interest rate which would have resulted in the recorded change. These are rates of change of percentage figures.

b. This is the difference between the 1968 white and nonwhite percentage figures.

Table 8

PERCENT OF OCCUPIED SUBSTANDARD HOUSING (BY REGION AND LOCATION) 1968

LOCATION	RACE	EVALUATION Percent in 1968	Size of White/ Nonwhite gap 1968
NORTH AND WEST[a]			
All housing units	W NW	5% 11%	6%
Central cities	W NW	4% 9%	5%
Suburban rings	W NW	3% 12%	9%
Nonmetropolitan areas	W NW	7% 22%	15%
SOUTH			
All housing units	W NW	9% 36%	27%
Central cities	W NW	3% 9%	6%
Suburban rings	W NW	3% 22%	19%
Nonmetropolitan areas	W NW	16% 61%	45%

Source of Data: *Social and Economic Status of Negroes in the United States, 1969,* p. 58.

a. Includes the entire United States except the South. (See Note 1, page 47.)

Table 9

MEDIAN YEARS OF SCHOOL COMPLETED BY PERSONS 20 YEARS OLD AND OVER (BY AGE), 1969

AGE GROUP	NUMBER OF SCHOOL YEARS COMPLETED		GAP
	Black	White	
20 and 21	12.2	12.8	.6
22 to 24	12.2	12.7	.5
25 to 29	12.1	12.6	.5
30 to 34	12.0	12.5	.5
35 to 44	10.6	12.4	1.8
45 to 54	9.1	12.2	3.1
55 to 64	7.6	10.9	3.3
65 to 74	6.1	8.9	2.8
75 and over	5.2	8.5	3.3

Source of Data: *Social and Economic Status of Negroes in the United States, 1969,* p. 50.

Table 10

MEDIAN INCOME FOR WHITE AND BLACK MALES 25-54 YEARS OF AGE (BY LOCATION AND YEARS OF SCHOOL COMPLETED), 1959-1967

LOCATION AND YEARS OF SCHOOL COMPLETED		DATA 1959	DATA 1967	Imputed annual rate of change 1959-1967[a]	Size of white/ black gap 1967	Percent change in gap size 1959-1967
CENTRAL CITIES						
Elementary	W	$5137	$5658	+1.2%	$1443	−15.5%
(8 years or less)	B	$3428	$4215	+2.6%		
High School	W	$5788	$6748	+2.0%	$1662	− 3.9%
(1-3 years)	B	$4059	$5086	+2.8%		
High School	W	$6265	$7543	+2.3%	$1901	− 2.1%
(4 years)	B	$4323	$5642	+3.4%		
College	W	$7686	$9222	+2.3%	$2197	−17.5%
(1 year or more)	B	$5022	$7025	+4.3%		
College	W	$8486	$10261	+2.4%	$2705	−
(4 yrs or more)	B	n.a.[b]	$7556	−		
SUBURBAN RINGS						
Elementary	W	$5507	$6454	+2.0%	$2433	−11.8%
(8 years or less)	B	$2750	$4021	+4.8%		
High School	W	$6342	$7495	+2.1%	$2864	+30.0%
(1-3 years)	B	$4050	$4631	+1.7%		
High School	W	$6774	$8188	+2.4%	$2208	− 9.5%
(4 years)	B	$4333	$5980	+4.0%		
College	W	$8726	$10499	+2.3%	$3179	−10.7%
(1 year or more)	B	$5167	$7320	+4.5%		
College	W	$9536	$11536	+2.4%	−	−
(4 yrs or more)	B	n.a.[b]	n.a.[b]	−		

Source of Data: U.S. Bureau of the Census, *Current Population Reports,* Series P-23, Special Studies (formerly Technical Studies), No. 27, "Trends in Social and Economic Conditions in Metropolitan Areas" (Washington, D.C.: U.S. Government Printing Office, 1969), p. 26.

a. This is the annual compound interest growth rate needed during 1959 to 1967 in order to account for the recorded change.

b. n.a. = not available

Table 11

BLACK MEDIAN INCOME AS A PERCENT OF WHITE MEDIAN INCOME (BY LOCATION AND YEARS OF SCHOOL COMPLETED), 1959–1967

	DATA		EVALUATION	
LOCATION AND YEARS OF SCHOOL COMPLETED	1959	1967	Magnitude of percentage change 1959-1967[a]	Imputed annual rate of change 1959-1967[b]
CENTRAL CITIES				
Elementary (8 years or less)	67%	75%	+8%	+1.4%
High school (1-3 years)	70%	75%	+5%	+0.9%
High school (4 years)	69%	75%	+6%	+1.1%
College (1 year or more)	65%	76%	+11%	+2.0%
College (4 years or more)	n.a.[c]	74%	—	—
SUBURBAN RINGS				
Elementary (8 years or less)	50%	62%	+12%	+2.7%
High school (1-3 years)	64%	62%	−2%	−0.4%
High school (4 years)	64%	73%	+9%	+1.7%
College (1 year or more)	59%	70%	+11%	+2.2%
College (4 years or more)	n.a.[c]	n.a.[c]	—	—

Source of Data: *Current Population Reports,* "Trends in Social and Economic Conditions in Metropolitan Areas," 1969, p. 26.

a. The difference in percentage is achieved by subtracting 1959 from 1967 figures.
b. This is the annual compound interest growth rate needed during 1959 to 1967 to account for the recorded change in percentages.
c. Not available.

Chapter 3

Income Distribution and Racial Equality

To enhance understanding of some of the data presented earlier, additional information about the generation and distribution of income is given here. The reason for focusing on income is not, of course, that it is the only important indicator of progress, but rather that there is fairly general agreement that more income is better than less and that income is related closely to other indicators of progress. In some cases, income is important in improving the levels of other indicators, as in health. In other cases, improvements in other indicators, such as education, can be expected to increase future income levels.

This discussion focuses on the complexities of relationships and influences with respect to income distribution and racial equality. It highlights the importance of viewing several indicators jointly for improved interpretations of some of the information given earlier. Three major topics are dealt with: 1) distribution of current income, comparing whites and nonwhites; 2) sources of current income for nonwhites; and 3) prospects for future income increases for nonwhites.

CURRENT INCOME DISTRIBUTION

Three income measures are used in this report: median family income, percent of persons below the poverty level, and percent of families with income greater than $8,000. They show how the distribution of income among blacks differs from that among whites. Nonwhites (see Table 1) are heavily represented in the low income groups while whites are heavily represented in the high income groups. Therefore, all of these measures must be considered in comparing progress of whites to that of nonwhites.

Earlier, attention was called to the different interpretations of data which result from looking only at the gap change or only at the difference in rates. Now, attention is called to the importance of considering the whole income distribution in evaluating the progress of nonwhites. Several important studies speak to this subject.

Lester Thurow[1] has demonstrated that high levels of national economic growth, low levels of national unemployment, and increased government purchases of goods and services have a relatively greater positive impact on median incomes of nonwhites than of whites. Since in the decade of the 1960's improvements occurred in these variables, they provide an explanation for the higher rate of improvement in median income levels for nonwhites relative to whites.

This explanation is also supported by Harold Guthrie of The Urban Institute.[2] He concludes:

1. In all segments of the income distribution, the unemployment rate is low when growth rates of income are higher among black families than among white families.

2. In the middle range of the income distribution, rising unemployment is more disadvantageous to black families than to white families.

3. At a stable 3.5 percent unemployment rate, equality of incomes for whites and blacks could be achieved in about 25 years.

4. If unemployment rises to a stable 4.5 percent rate, black families bear a social cost that can be measured in terms of the additional time required to achieve equality—an additional 25 years, or 50 years hence.

5. During a period when incomes of black families are growing more rapidly than the incomes of white families, the absolute differences, or gap, will increase to a maximum and then decline, posing an apparent paradox that can be explained by a growth-unemployment model.

This latter point implies that a continuation of rapid economic growth and low unemployment rates could lead to an eventual decline in the gap between white and nonwhite median income levels.

1. Lester C. Thurow, "Analysing the American Income Distribution," paper presented at the American Economic Association Meeting, July 11, 1969.
2. Harold W. Guthrie, "The Prospect for Equality of Incomes between White and Black Families under Varying Rates of Unemployment," *The Journal of Human Resources*, Vol. V, No. 4 (Fall, 1970), 431-446. The conclusions cited in the text are based upon estimates from the growth-unemployment model described in more detail in this reference.

Research done by Donald Tucker[3] has shown that much of the recent improvement in median income levels for nonwhites is largely attributable to income improvements in lower income groups of both whites and nonwhites. This has more impact on the nonwhite median than on the white median since whites tend to enjoy more representation in high income groups and nonwhites tend to be over-represented in the lower income groups. Tucker's research supports the conclusion that the pressure of rapid economic growth and low national unemployment rates will be even more essential in the future if nonwhites, as they move increasingly into the middle income groups, are to maintain the same rates of improvement.

SOURCES OF CURRENT INCOME

The studies briefly described call attention to the critical importance of earned income—wages and salaries—to the nonwhite population. Their relative gains are dependent upon high levels of employment, upgrading, and promotion. The special importance of earned income to nonwhites is due to their relatively lower incomes than whites from profits, interest, and dividends. It is crucial, therefore, to look at prospects for improving levels of earned income.

It is well documented that a nonwhite labor force member has a higher probability of being unemployed than if he were white. The nonwhite unemployment rate tends to be about twice that for whites. This is attributable to a wide variety of possible causes. Among the most important is the over-representation of nonwhites in those occupations characterized by lower wages and higher unemployment rates. This may be seen in Table 12 which shows occupational distributions for the white and nonwhite labor force in 1960 and 1968 along with the respective unemployment rates. Note that the 1968 unemployment rate for white-collar workers—accounting for 49.5 percent of whites and 24.4 percent of nonwhites—was less than half of that for blue-collar workers—with 35.5 percent whites and 42.4 percent nonwhites. Service workers—comprised of 28.3 percent of nonwhites and only 10.4 percent of whites—also had about twice the white-collar unemployment rate.

The fact that nonwhites tend to earn less in most occupations than whites in the same occupations is another aspect of differentials in earnings. Table 13 provides data on the median earnings and employment distribution (percent of nonwhites and whites in each occupation) of nonwhite and white males in central cities in 1967. Note that in all occupations nonwhites earned less than their white counterparts. Since the occupational categories are very broad it is probable that salary variations are attributable both to the many

---

3. Donald P. Tucker, "Intra-Firm Earnings Mobility of Whites and Nonwhites: 1962-1966," UI Working Paper 113-36 (Washington, D.C.: The Urban Institute, 1970)

types of jobs within a given category and to inequalities in salaries and wages. Table 14, based in part on the information in Table 13, summarizes the effects of both the occupational and earnings disparities between white and nonwhite males. For example, nonwhite males would have earned 45 percent more had their occupational distribution and earnings rate within occupations been that of white males.

FUTURE INCOME IMPROVEMENTS

In addition to the factors mentioned above, prospects for future income improvements for nonwhites depend upon current investments to encourage their migration to higher income areas, education, and employment related training.

Richard Wertheimer has investigated differences in income attributable to migration within the United States.[4] He finds that among migrants from rural areas to urban areas, as compared to nonmigrants, nonwhites tend to obtain absolute income improvements and relatively greater improvements than whites. This finding helps in assessing the significance of the population trends described in Chapter 4.

Increased levels of education on the average result in increased income levels in future years for both nonwhites and whites. Therefore, the increases in percent of people completing high school and college shown in Table 2 should lead to income improvements for both groups. The net effect of these factors on relative income changes between whites and nonwhites is more difficult to assess. The imputed rate of increase for nonwhites is higher than for whites in both cases, but the gap for those completing college has increased.

There is a further difficulty. Nonwhites have tended to achieve less future income improvement from each additional year's education than have whites. Lester Thurow[5] has shown, using 1960 data, that nonwhites with the same number of years of work experience as whites consistently get lower income gains from education than whites and that these disparities tend to increase at higher levels of education. If this pattern persists, the increasing size of the white/nonwhite gap for those completing four years of college[6] will lead to a continuation and possible expansion of the overall income gaps between whites and nonwhites. This could be so in spite of the absolute increases attributable to more education for both groups.

4. Richard F. Wertheimer II, *The Monetary Rewards of Migration within the U.S.* (Washington, D.C.: The Urban Institute, 1970).

5. Lester C. Thurow, "The Occupational Distribution of the Returns to Education and Experience for Whites and Negroes," in *Federal Programs for the Development of Human Resources,* the Subcommittee on Economic Progress of the Joint Economic Committee, Congress of the United States (Washington, D.C.: Government Printing Office, 1968).

6. See Table 2: 9.0 percent gap in 1968 versus 7.4 percent gap in 1960.

In the latter half of the 1960's the Department of Labor engaged in a significant reorientation of manpower training efforts in the direction of the disadvantaged. One effect of this has been an increased attempt to provide training for the nonwhite population. Unfortunately, it is impossible at this stage to estimate the effect of this increased training on nonwhite incomes because of the ambiguous results of training program evaluations. Nevertheless, the shift in emphasis toward the disadvantaged has meant that more nonwhites have been receiving greater manpower development services than previously. The net effect of this shift should be to improve nonwhite employment prospects and, therefore, to improve their future income prospects.

In conclusion, important improvements in each of the areas discussed are noted during the 1960 to 1968 period. Nonwhite income levels were significantly raised and the prospects for narrowing the white/nonwhite income gap will certainly be enhanced if nonwhites continue to move into higher paying occupations with lower unemployment rates. In addition, emphasis on training the disadvantaged, the increased participation of nonwhites in higher education, and their migration to urban areas can all be expected to lead to higher incomes. However, equality of income distribution, rising wages and salaries, and special programs to improve future income for nonwhites have all been dependent upon rapid rates of economic growth and low national unemployment rates, both of which conditions existed during the decade of the 1960's. There is, therefore, little ground for optimism or complacency if the national growth rates decline and unemployment rates rise, as they did in 1970, unless alternative means are found to narrow the income gaps.[7] The effect of such a deteriorating situation will be relatively more serious for nonwhites than for whites and the gains seen may well be lost in a period of economic decline.

7. The likelihood of narrowing the gaps would be enhanced by a more satisfactory resolution of the problem of the association of low unemployment rates with rapid price increases. On this see Charles C. Holt, C. D. MacRae, S. O. Schweitzer and R. E. Smith, *The Unemployment-Inflation Dilemma: A Manpower Solution* (Washington, D.C.: The Urban Institute, 1971).

Table 12.

OCCUPATIONAL DISTRIBUTION AMONG WHITES AND NONWHITES AND UNEMPLOYMENT RATES: 1960–1968

OCCUPATION		WHITE/NONWHITE OCCUPATIONAL DISTRIBUTION 1960	1968	UNEMPLOYMENT RATES[a] 1960	1968
TOTAL EMPLOYED (millions)	W NW	59,637 7,045	67,751 8,169	5.5%	3.6%
WHITE-COLLAR WORKERS	W NW	46.3% 16.0	49.5% 24.4	2.7%	2.0%
Professional and Technical	W NW	12.0 4.7	14.3 7.8	1.7	1.2
Managers, officials and proprietors	W NW	11.6 2.5	11.1 2.8	1.4	1.0
Clerical workers	W NW	15.6 7.2	17.5 11.8	3.8	3.0
Sales workers	W NW	7.2 1.6	6.6 1.9	3.8	2.8
BLUE-COLLAR WORKERS	W NW	35.9% 39.8	35.5% 42.4	7.8	4.1
Craftsmen and foremen	W NW	13.7 5.9	13.8 8.0	5.3	2.4
Operatives	W NW	17.7 20.1	17.7 23.7	8.0	4.5
Nonfarm laborers	W NW	4.5 13.8	4.0 10.7	12.6	7.2
SERVICE WORKERS	W NW	10.3% 31.7	10.4% 28.3	5.8	4.4
FARMERS AND FARM LABORERS	W NW	7.6% 12.4	4.5% 4.9	3.9	2.1

Sources of Data: Occupational distribution data: U.S. Department of Labor, Bureau of Labor Statistics, 1969; unemployment rates: Bureau of Labor Statistics, 1970; and median income data: U.S. Department of Commerce, Bureau of the Census, *Current Population Reports,* Series P-60.

a. Includes whites and nonwhites.

Table 13

MEDIAN EARNINGS AND DISTRIBUTION BY OCCUPATION OF MALE FULL-TIME EMPLOYEES IN CENTRAL CITIES, 1967–1968

OCCUPATION	RACE	MEDIAN EARNINGS 1967	OCCUPATIONAL DISTRIBUTION[a] 1968
Professional and managerial workers	W	$9,542	30%
	NW	6,208	9
Clerical and sales workers	W	6,878	17
	NW	5,515	12
Craftsmen and foremen	W	7,545	21
	NW	5,962	13
Operatives	W	6,475	19
	NW	5,414	32
Nonfarm laborers	W	5,355	5
	NW	4,492	17
Service workers, except private household	W	5,536	8
	NW	4,159	17

Source of Data: *Current Population Reports,* "Trends in Social and Economic Conditions in Metropolitan Areas," 1969, pp. 33 and 49.

a. These figures indicate that, in the first category, 30 percent of all white males and 9 percent of all nonwhite males held professional or managerial positions in central cities in 1968, and so forth.

Table 14

EFFECTS OF OCCUPATIONAL AND EARNING DISPARITIES BETWEEN WHITE AND BLACK MALES, 1966–1967

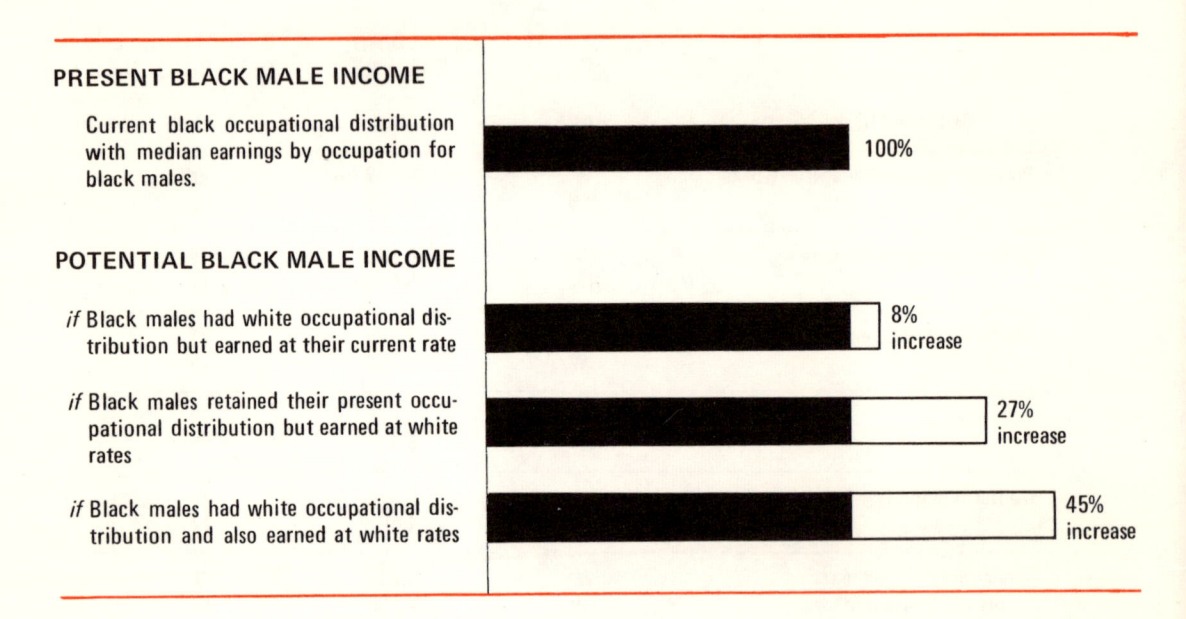

PRESENT BLACK MALE INCOME

Current black occupational distribution with median earnings by occupation for black males. — 100%

POTENTIAL BLACK MALE INCOME

if Black males had white occupational distribution but earned at their current rate — 8% increase

if Black males retained their present occupational distribution but earned at white rates — 27% increase

if Black males had white occupational distribution and also earned at white rates — 45% increase

Source: Calculated using data from Table 13.

Chapter 4

White and Black Population Trends

This chapter, providing the demographic background to the rest of the report, presents recent white and black population trends in the United States. The data are given in a series of tables and cover the 1960 decade, although there was some variation in the years for which the data were collected.

Following are some of the crucial implications that appear in the data:

Table 15: The proportion of all blacks living in the South[1] is declining, while the proportion is rising in other regions of the country. However, more than half of all blacks still live in the South.

Table 16: Despite the changes indicated in the previous table, blacks are still about 20 percent of the population of the South and less than 10 percent elsewhere.

Table 17: There was a substantial growth in the suburban white populations of the metropolitan areas in all four regions, while the central city white population declined in all but the Western region. The high percentage growth rate of the suburban black population is due largely to its small initial population at the start of the decade. In the West only, the numerical growth of the black population was greater in the suburban rings than in the central cities.

Table 18: The proportion of blacks in the total population of the Northcentral and Northeastern central cities rose to 23 percent and 18

---

1. The standard census definition for the South is used here. This includes the states of the Old Confederacy as well as Delaware, the District of Columbia, Kentucky, Maryland, Oklahoma and West Virginia.

percent respectively, which is an increase of about one-third. There was a slight increase to 27 percent and 10 percent respectively in the Southern and Western central cities. The proportion of blacks in the suburbs remained stable at about 3 percent in the Northeast and the Northcentral regions, while it declined from 12 percent to 10 percent in the South, and doubled to 4 percent in the West.

Table 19: The proportion of all blacks living in central cities of larger metropolitan areas has risen from 30 percent to 34 percent while the proportion dropped from 21 percent to 20 percent in central cities of smaller metropolitan areas. While 54 percent of the blacks live in central cities, only 26 percent of the whites do and, of these, exactly one-half (13 percent) live in larger cities and one-half in smaller cities.

Table 20: An examination of the percent of blacks in the total population of the thirty largest cities shows that Washington, Newark, and Atlanta had the highest percentages in 1967, and that Washington and Newark also showed the largest change in percentage figures from 1960 to 1967. The percentage figures for 1950 have been included to give additional perspective to the changes in the last decade. The 1970 Census figures will undoubtedly show that a number of additional cities are now more than 50 percent black.

Table 21: Blacks comprise 25 percent of the total population of the larger central cities and only 16 percent of the smaller central cities' population. The growth of the proportion of blacks in the population of the larger cities is over twice that of the smaller cities. The proportion of blacks living in the suburbs of both small and large metropolitan areas is remaining about the same.

Table 22: The black population is younger than the white population. The percentage difference between the white and black figures is largest under 13 years and over 45 years of age.[2]

Table 23: In the central cities of metropolitan areas the white and black age differences are even more pronounced and are tending to grow larger.

Table 24: An average of 34 percent of the under-16 population of our largest cities are black and this figure is growing more rapidly than any other.

---

2. There is a 5 percentage point difference between the percent of whites and blacks in the 5-13 age group, and between the percent of white and black males in the 45-54 age group.

Table 15

PERCENT OF THE TOTAL BLACK POPULATION LIVING IN EACH REGION OF THE UNITED STATES, 1960–1969

	DATA		EVALUATION	
REGION	1960	1969	Magnitude of change in percentages 1960-1969[a]	Imputed annual rate of change of percentages 1960-1969[b]
South	60%	52%	−8%	−1.6%
Northeast	16%	19%	+3%	+1.9%
North Central	18%	21%	+3%	+1.7%
West	6%	7%	+1%	+1.7%

Source of Data: *The Social and Economic Status of Negroes in the United States, 1969,* p. 3. Percentages may not always add to totals, because of rounding.

a. This is the difference in percentages (a subtraction process) between the years covered. It does not represent the change in total population, only the change in the percentages.

b. This is the annual compound interest rate required to achieve the recorded changes in the percentages. It is a method of quantifying differing rates of change in these percentage figures.

Table 16

BLACKS AS A PERCENT OF THE TOTAL POPULATION OF THE UNITED STATES AND OF EACH REGION, 1960–1969

REGION	DATA 1960	DATA 1969	Magnitude of change in percentages 1960-1969[a]	Imputed annual rate of change of percentages 1960-1969[b]
United States	11%	11%	0	0.0
South	21%	19%	−2%	−1.1%
Northeast	7%	9%	+2%	+2.8%
North Central	7%	8%	+1%	+1.5%
West	4%	5%	+1%	+2.5%

Source of Data: *The Social and Economic Status of Negroes in the United States, 1969*, p. 4.

a. The 1960 percentage is subtracted from the 1969 percentage to obtain the magnitude of change.

b. This is the annual compound interest rate required to achieve the recorded changes in the percentages. It is a method of quantifying rates of change in these percentage figures.

Table 17

PERCENT OF POPULATION IN CENTRAL CITIES AND SUBURBS (BY REGION) 1960–1968

		DATA		EVALUATION	
		Population (in millions)		Magnitude of change (in millions)	Annual rate of change in population
REGION	RACE	1960	1968	1960-1968	1960-1968 [a]
UNITED STATES	W	158.7	174.0	+15.3	+1.1%
	B	18.4	22.0	+3.6	+2.2%
NORTHEAST					
Central cities	W	15.0	13.5	−1.5	−1.3%
	B	2.3	3.0	+.7	+3.3%
Suburban rings	W	17.6	20.1	+2.5	+1.6%
	B	.6	.7	+.1	+2.0%
NORTH CENTRAL					
Central cities	W	13.5	12.9	−.6	− .6%
	B	2.7	3.8	+1.1	+4.2%
Suburban rings	W	14.1	17.6	+3.5	+3.0%
	B	.3	.5	+.2	+6.6%
SOUTH					
Central cities	W	11.1	10.8	−.3	−0.4%
	B	3.7	4.1	+.4	+1.2%
Suburban rings	W	9.9	14.2	+4.3	+4.6%
	B	1.4	1.6	+.2	+1.7%
WEST					
Central cities	W	8.0	8.2	+.2	+ .3%
	B	.7	.9	+.2	+3.5%
Suburban rings	W	10.3	14.0	+3.7	+4.2%
	B	.2	.5	+.3	+11.5%

Source of Data: *Current Population Reports,* "Trends in Social and Economic Conditions in Metropolitan Areas," 1969, p. 6. Data were rounded off after calculations, so calculations do not always match figures in the table.

[a] This is the annual compound interest growth rate needed during 1960 to 1968 to account for the recorded changes.

Table 18

BLACKS AS A PERCENT OF TOTAL POPULATION OF CENTRAL CITIES AND SUBURBS (BY REGION), 1960–1968

| | DATA || EVALUATION ||
REGION	Percent of total population 1960	1968	Magnitude of change of percentages 1960-1968	Imputed annual rate of change of percentages 1960-1968[a]
NORTHEAST				
Central cities	13%	18%	+5%	+4.1%
Suburban rings	3%	3%	0	0.0%
NORTH CENTRAL				
Central cities	17%	23%	+5%	+3.8%
Suburban rings	2%	3%	+1%	+5.2%
SOUTH				
Central cities	25%	27%	+2%	+0.97%
Suburban rings	12%	10%	−2%	−2.2%
WEST				
Central cities	8%	10%	+2%	+2.8%
Suburban rings	2%	4%	+2%	+9.0%

Source of Data: *Current Population Reports,* "Trends in Social and Economic Conditions in Metropolitan Areas," 1969, p. 7.

a. This is the annual compound interest rate required to achieve the recorded changes in the percentages. It is a method of quantifying differing rates of change in these percentage figures.

Table 19

PERCENT OF BLACKS AND WHITES IN CENTRAL CITIES AND SUBURBS (BY SIZE): 1960–1968

		DATA		EVALUATION	
REGION	RACE	1960	1968	Magnitude of change in percentages 1960-1968[a]	Imputed annual rate of change of percentages 1960-1968[b]
IN METROPOLITAN AREAS OF ONE MILLION OR MORE					
Central cities	W	15%	13%	−2%	−1.8%
	B	30%	34%	+4%	+1.6%
Suburban rings	W	19%	22%	+3%	+1.9%
	B	7%	8%	+1%	+1.7%
IN METROPOLITAN AREAS UNDER ONE MILLION					
Central cities	W	15%	13%	−2%	−1.8%
	B	21%	20%	−1%	−0.6%
Suburban rings	W	14%	16%	+2%	+1.7%
	B	7%	7%	0.0%	0.0%
OUTSIDE METROPOLITAN AREAS					
	W	37%	36%	−1%	−0.3%
	B	35%	31%	−4%	−1.6%

Source of Data: *Current Population Reports,* "Trends in Social and Economic Conditions in Metropolitan Areas," 1969, p. 4. These figures are the percentages of the U.S. white (or black) population living in the large or small cities and suburbs.

a. The difference in percentages (a subtraction process) between the percentage of all blacks living in each type of residence between the years 1960 and 1968.

b. This is the annual compound interest rate required to achieve the recorded changes in the percentages. It is a method for quantifying rates of change in percentage figures.

Table 20

PERCENT OF BLACKS IN THE TOTAL POPULATION OF EACH OF THE THIRTY LARGEST CITIES: 1950–1967

		DATA			EVALUATION	
SIZE RANKING[a]	CITY[b]	Percent of Blacks 1950	1960	1967	Magnitude of change of percentages 1960-1967	Imputed annual rate of change of percentages 1960-1967[c]
9	Washington, D.C.	35%	54%	69%	+15%	+3.6%
30	Newark	17	34	49	+15	+5.3
24	Atlanta	37	38	44	+6	+2.1
6	Baltimore	24	35	41	+6	+2.3
15	New Orleans	32	37	41	+4	+1.5
22	Memphis	37%	37%	40%	+3%	+1.1%
5	Detroit	16	29	39	+10	+4.3
10	St. Louis	18	29	37	+8	+3.6
8	Cleveland	16	29	34	+5	+2.3
4	Philadelphia	18	26	33	+7	+3.5
2	Chicago	14%	23%	30%	+7%	+3.8%
21	Cincinnati	16	22	24	+2	+1.3
26	Indianapolis	15	21	24	+3	+1.9
27	Kansas City	12	18	22	+4	+2.9
7	Houston	21	23	22	−1	−0.6

Source of Data: *Current Population Reports,* "Trends in Social and Economic Conditions in Metropolitan Areas," 1969, p. 9. The percentage figures for 1950 have been included to give additional perspective to the changes in the last decade.

a. Largest size is ranked #1. These are 1960 size rankings before 1970 census data were available.

		DATA			EVALUATION	
SIZE RANKING[a]	CITY[b]	Percent of Blacks			Magnitude of change of percentages 1960-1967	Imputed annual rate of change of percentages 1960-1967[c]
		1950	1960	1967		
14	Dallas	13%	19%	22%	+3%	+2.4%
16	Pittsburgh	12	17	21	+4	+3.1
1	New York	10	14	19	+5	+4.5
28	Columbus	12	16	19	+3	+2.5
3	Los Angeles	9	14	18	+4	+3.6
20	Buffalo	6%	13%	17%	+4%	+3.9%
13	Boston	5	9	15	+6	+7.5
11	Milwaukee	3	8	14	+6	+8.3
12	San Francisco	6	10	14	+4	+4.9
23	Denver	4	6	9	+3	+6.0
17	San Antonio	7%	7%	8%	+1%	+1.9%
18	San Diego	5	6	7	+1	+2.2
19	Seattle	3	5	7	+2	+4.9
29	Phoenix	5	5	5	0	0.0
25	Minneapolis	1	2	4	+2	+10.4

b. Arranged in order of estimated percentage of blacks in 1967. The 1970 Census figures will undoubtedly show that a number of additional cities are now more than 50 percent black.

c. This is the annual compound interest rate required to account for the recorded change in the proportion of blacks in the total population between 1960 and 1968.

Table 21

BLACKS AS A PERCENT OF THE TOTAL POPULATION IN CENTRAL CITIES AND SUBURBS (BY SIZE): 1960–1968

	DATA		EVALUATION	
REGION	1960	1968	Magnitude of change of percentages 1960-1968[a]	Imputed annual rate of change of percentages 1960-1968[b]
IN METROPOLITAN AREAS ONE MILLION OR MORE				
Central cities	18%	25%	+7%	+4.2%
Suburban rings	4%	4%	0	0
IN METROPOLITAN AREAS UNDER ONE MILLION				
Central cities	14%	16%	+2%	+1.7%
Suburban rings	5%	5%	0	0

Source of Data: *Current Population Reports,* "Trends in Social and Economic Conditions in Metropolitan Areas," 1969, p. 5.

a. This is the difference in percentages (a subtraction process) between the percent of blacks in the total population of these cities and suburbs in 1960 and 1969.

b. This is the annual compound interest rate required to achieve the recorded changes in the percentages. It is a method of quantifying rates of change in these percentage figures.

Table 22

PERCENT OF WHITE AND BLACK POPULATION IN THE UNITED STATES BY AGE AND SEX, 1969

AGE	RACE	MALE Percent of total Population	FEMALE Percent of total Population
All ages	W B	100% 100%	100% 100%
Under 5 years	W B	9% 13%	8% 12%
5–13 years	W B	19% 24%	17% 22%
14–15 years	W B	4% 5%	4% 4%
16–19 years	W B	7% 8%	7% 8%
20–24 years	W B	7% 7%	8% 8%
25–34 years	W B	12% 11%	12% 12%
35–44 years	W B	12% 10%	12% 11%
45–64 years	W B	21% 16%	21% 17%
65 years and over	W B	9% 6%	11% 7%
Median age	W B	28.2 yrs. 19.8 yrs.	30.3 yrs. 22.4 yrs.

Source of Data: *The Social and Economic Status of Negroes in the United States, 1969,* p. 11.

Table 23

PERCENT OF POPULATION BY AGE IN CENTRAL CITIES, 1960–1968

		DATA		EVALUATION	
AGE	RACE	1960	1968	Magnitude of change in percentages 1960-1968[a]	Imputed annual rate of change of percentages 1960-1968[b]
All ages	W	100%	100%		
	B	100%	100%		
Under 5 years	W	10%	8%	–2%	–2.8%
	B	14%	13%	–1%	–0.9%
5–15 years	W	18%	19%	+1%	+0.7%
	B	23%	27%	+4%	+2.0%
16–19 years	W	5%	7%	+2%	+4.3%
	B	6%	8%	+2%	+3.6%
20–24 years	W	7%	8%	+1%	+1.6%
	B	7%	7%	0%	0.0%
25–44 years	W	26%	23%	–3%	–1.5%
	B	29%	24%	–5%	–2.4%
45–64 years	W	23%	23%	0.0%	0.0%
	B	17%	16%	–1%	–0.8%
65 years and over	W	11%	13%	+2%	+2.1%
	B	5%	5%	0%	0.0%
Median age	W	32.5 yrs.	32.3 yrs.	+0.2 yrs.	+0.8%
	B	25.6 yrs.	21.7 yrs.	–3.9 yrs.	–2.0%

Source of Data: *Current Population Reports,* "Trends in Social and Economic Conditions in Metropolitan Areas," 1969, p. 8. Percentages may not always add to totals, because of rounding.

a. This is the difference in percentage figures (subtraction) between the data for 1960 and 1968.

b. This is the annual compound interest rate required to account for the recorded change in the percentage of the population in the particular age group during the years 1960–1968.

Table 24

BLACKS AS A PERCENT OF TOTAL POPULATION IN CENTRAL CITIES BY AGE, 1960–1968

AGE	DATA 1960	DATA 1968	Magnitude of change in percentages 1960-1968[a]	Imputed annual rate of change in percentages 1960-1968[b]
Blacks of all ages				
G1M[c]	18%	25%	+7%	+4.2%
L1M	14%	16%	+2%	+1.7%
Under 16 years				
G1M	23%[d]	34%	+11%	+5.0%
L1M	18%	21%	+3%	+1.9%
16–19 years				
G1M	20%	28%	+8%	+4.2%
L1M	16%	18%	+2%	+1.5%
20–24 years				
G1M	20%	23%	+3%	+1.8%
L1M	12%	15%	+3%	+2.8%
25–64 years				
G1M	17%	22%	+5%	+3.2%
L1M	13%	14%	+1%	+1.0%
65 years and over				
G1M	10%	10%	0%	0%
L1M	8%	8%	0%	0%

Source of Data: *Current Population Reports,* "Trends in Social and Economic Conditions in Metropolitan Areas," 1969, p. 10.

a. This is the difference in percentage figures (subtraction) between the population data for 1960 and 1968.

b. This is the annual compound interest rate required to account for the recorded change in the percentage of blacks in the central cities during 1960–1968.

c. G1M = Central cities in metropolitan areas of greater than 1 million population; L1M = Central cities in metropolitan areas of less than 1 million population.

d. That is, of the under-16 G1M population, 23% were black, and so forth.

Appendix A

A Tabulation of Indicators with Formulas and Sample Calculations

Table 25 tabulates the measures presented in Tables 2–4 (Chapter 1) as well as several other more sophisticated measures that could be used as aids in understanding the implications of the 1960 and 1968 racial data. It will be found on pages 68 to 75.

A detailed explanation of this table is presented here with a verbal description, the formula used, and a sample calculation for each of the measures or columns.

Table 26 then presents a ranking analysis of the measures tabulated in Table 25.

Column 3: *Imputed Annual Rate of Change: 1960-1968*

The imputed annual rate of change applies the compound interest formula to the 1960 and 1968 data, treating the white and nonwhite figures separately. It estimates the annual rate of compound interest that *would* have been required to cause the observed 1960-1968 changes in value. It is called the "imputed" rate because the data did not actually vary in such a uniform manner between 1960 and 1968.

Formula:[1]

$$(1 + \text{annual rate}) = \left(\frac{1968 \text{ value}}{1960 \text{ value}}\right)^{1/8}$$

Example (median income):[2]

$$(1 + \text{annual rate}) = \left(\frac{8937}{6857}\right)^{1/8} = (1.30)^{1/8} = 1.034$$

$$\text{interest rate} = 3.4\%$$

Column 4: *Difference in Imputed Rates of Change: 1960-1968*

The differences between the white and nonwhite rates of change in Column 3 are given in Column 4 as indicators of the comparative rates of change. A plus sign implies that the trends in the white and nonwhite data are such that eventually the difference will tend to decrease. These figures are ranked, with # 1 having the greatest tendency toward convergence.

The "% Teenagers unemployed" is ranked # 16 because this indicator shows the largest negative difference in white and nonwhite rates of change, −2.8%, (−6.7% minus −3.9%), and the difference is in a direction which tends to increase the gap. By comparison, the "% Illegitimate births" is ranked #1 because the rate of change for whites is much greater than that for nonwhites, and this condition will eventually tend to lessen the size of the gap.[3]

Formula:[4]

Difference = Nonwhite rate − White rate

Example (median income):

Difference = 4.9%−3.4% = +1.5%

1. The applicable compound interest formula is:

   Sum = Principal (1+ interest rate)^{number of years}

The imputed rate of change is equal to the interest rate.

2. This example shows the calculations for determining the imputed annual rate of change for whites.

3. Because of the greater value of the nonwhite level, the white/nonwhite gap is still getting larger (Column 6) despite the tendency towards convergence by the rates of change.

4. This is calculated so that a plus value is obtained when the rates tend to decrease white/nonwhite differences.

A TABULATION OF INDICATORS

Column 5: *Size of White/Nonwhite Gap: 1968*

                Considered together with

Column 6: *Percent Change in Size of White/Nonwhite Gap: 1960-1968*

Many of the figures for the "size of the white/nonwhite gap" (Column 5) are differences in percentages, rather than in absolute values.

To assist the reader in interpreting these changing figures, the absolute differences between them for different years (Column 5) was tabulated as well as the percentage change in these percentage figures for the same years (Column 6).

Formula (Column 5):

Gap = 1968 White level − 1968 Nonwhite level

Example (median income):

Gap size = $8937 − $5590 = $3347

Formula (Column 6):

$$\% \text{ Change} = \frac{1968 \text{ Gap size} - 1960 \text{ Gap size}}{1960 \text{ Gap size}}$$

Example (median income):

$$\% = \frac{\$3347 - \$3063}{\$3063} = +9.27\%$$

Column 7: *Normalized Gap: 1968*

The normalized gap is a composite indicator which reflects both the difference in the rate of change as well as the change in the size of the gap. It is calculated by dividing the white/nonwhite gap size by the average of the white and nonwhite levels for the year in question.[5] This was found to be the best measure taking into account trends in gap size as well as rates of change. The measure is also useful in comparing the relative magnitude of

---

5. This can be expressed as: Normalized Gap = $2\left(\frac{W-NW}{W+NW}\right)$ where W and NW are the white and nonwhite levels for the year in question.

the differences between the white and nonwhite levels for different socio-economic variables for any given years.[6]

Formula:

$$1968 \text{ Normalized Gap} = \frac{1968 \text{ White/Nonwhite gap}}{\frac{1968 \text{ White level} + 1968 \text{ Nonwhite level}}{2}}$$

Example (median income):

$$\text{Normalized Gap} = \frac{\$8937 - \$5590}{\frac{\$8937 + \$5590}{2}} = \frac{\$3347}{\$7264} = .461$$

Column 8: *Percent Change in Normalized Gap: 1960-1968*

The change in the normalized gap between 1960 and 1968 is a composite measure of the changes in the data over this time period. The indicator showing the largest increase in the normalized gap size (percent children living with two parents = +40%) is ranked 16 because it indicates the greatest increase in this measure of the white/nonwhite differences.

Formula:

$$\% \text{ Change} = \frac{1968 \text{ Normalized Gap} - 1960 \text{ Normalized Gap}}{1960 \text{ Normalized Gap}}$$

Example (median income):

$$\% \text{ Change} = \frac{.461 - .575}{.575} = -19.8\%$$

Column 9: *Minimum Required Annual Nonwhite Rate Resulting in a Reduction of the Gap Size in 1969*
Considered together with
Column 10: *1960-1968 Nonwhite Rate as a Percent of Required Rate*
(3) ÷ (9)

These columns show the nonwhite rate of improvement needed to reduce the size of the gap providing the white rate of change remains the same. This rate is determined on the basis of both the white and nonwhite levels and the white rate of change. Using income as an example, if A earns $16,000 a year and receives a 5% raise ($800), and B earns $10,000 a year, B needs at least an 8% raise ($800) in order to keep the dollar gap between the two salaries from growing.

6. Using a white/nonwhite ratio or its reciprocal for all cases is not satisfactory because sometimes the nonwhite level is larger (e.g., % illegitimate births). Dividing the gap size by the average of the two values is a more consistent and less biased way of comparing differences between white and nonwhite levels over several different socio-economic variables.

A TABULATION OF INDICATORS 65

Column 9 specifies the annual nonwhite growth rate required to begin decreasing the magnitude of the white/nonwhite gap providing the white rate of change stays the same. Column 10 divides the nonwhite 1960-1968 *imputed* annual rate of change (Column 3) by the *required* rate of change (Column 9). Percentage figures greater than 100% indicate the gap should begin to close if the present white and nonwhite rates of change remain the same. The indicator with the highest percentage figure is ranked 1 because it indicates the greatest tendency toward reduction of the gap.

Formula (Column 9):

$$\text{Required Nonwhite rate} = \frac{\text{1968 White level}}{\text{1968 Nonwhite level}} \times \text{1968 White rate}$$

Example (median income):

$$\text{Required rate} = \frac{\$8937}{\$5590} \times 3.4 = 5.44\%$$

Formula (Column 10):

$$\% \text{ of Required rate} = \frac{\text{1960-1968 Nonwhite rate}}{\text{Required rate to reduce the gap}}$$

Example (median income):

$$\% = \frac{4.9}{5.44} = 90.13\%$$

Column 11: *Year Nonwhites May Reach 1968 White Level*

This column gives the year nonwhites might reach 1968 white levels were the nonwhite annual imputed rates of change (Column 3) to remain the same. Since the rates are unlikely to remain the same, these estimates *are not a prediction* but only another means of understanding the 1960-1968 data.

Formula:

$$\text{Year} = 1968 + \left(\frac{\log\left(\frac{\text{1968 white level}}{\text{1968 nonwhite level}}\right)}{\log(1 + \text{nonwhite rate})} \right)$$

Example: (median income):

$$\text{Year} = 1968 + \frac{\log 1.6}{\log 1.049} = 1968 + \frac{.203}{.0208}$$

Year to reach 1968 level = 1968 + 9.76 = 1977.76

Column 12: *Required Annual Nonwhite Rate for Nonwhites to Reach 1968 White Level by 1976*
Considered together with
Column 13: *1960-1968 Nonwhite Rate as a Percent of Required Rate (3) ÷ (12)*

A slightly different question is posed in Column 12: What annual nonwhite rate of change would be required for nonwhites to reach 1968 white levels by 1976? In Column 13, the imputed nonwhite rate of change for 1960-68 (Column 3) is divided by the required rate (Column 12).

Formula (Column 12):[7]

$$\log(1 + \text{required rate}) = \frac{\log\left(\frac{1968 \text{ White level}}{1968 \text{ Nonwhite level}}\right)}{8}$$

Example (median income):

$$\log(1 + \text{required rate}) = \frac{\log 1.6}{8}$$

$$\log(1 + \text{required rate}) = \frac{.203}{8} = .0255$$

$$1 + \text{required rate} = 1.06$$

$$\text{Required rate} = 6\%$$

Formula (Column 13):

$$\% \text{ of required rate} = \frac{\text{Imputed annual Nonwhite rate}}{\text{Required rate}}$$

Example (median income):

$$\% = \frac{4.9}{6.0} = 81.66\%$$

Column 14: *Possible Percent Change in White/Nonwhite Gap Size: 1968-1976*
Considered together with
Column 15: *Possible Percent Change in Normalized Gap: 1968-1976*

Assuming that the 1960-1968 imputed annual rates of change for whites and nonwhites (Column 3) remain the same until 1976, Column 14 presents the percentage change in the white/nonwhite gap size from 1968-1976, and Column 15 gives a similar percentage calculation for the normalized gap. Again, this is not a *prediction*, but rather a *projection* of current data.

---

7. The applicable compound interest formula is:

$$\text{Sum} = \text{Principal}(1 + \text{interest rate})^{\text{number of years}}$$

A TABULATION OF INDICATORS

Formulas (Column 14):[8]

$$\text{White 1976 level} = \text{1968 level} \times \frac{\text{1968 level}}{\text{1960 level}}$$

$$\text{Nonwhite 1976 level} = \text{1968 level} \times \frac{\text{1968 level}}{\text{1960 level}}$$

1976 Gap = 1976 White level − 1976 Nonwhite level

$$\text{\% Change} = \frac{\text{1976 gap} - \text{1968 gap}}{\text{1968 gap}}$$

Example (median income):

1976 White level = $8937 × 1.30 = $11,645

1976 Nonwhite level = $5590 × 1.47 = $8,217

1976 Gap = $11,645 − $8,217 = $3428

$$\text{\% Change in gap} = \frac{\$3428 - \$3347}{\$3347} = +2.4\%$$

Formulas (Column 15):

Calculate 1976 White and Nonwhite levels and 1976 Gap as in Column 14 previous.

$$\text{1976 Average} = \frac{(\text{1976 White level} + \text{1976 Nonwhite level})}{2}$$

$$\text{1976 Normalized Gap} = \frac{\text{1976 Gap}}{\text{1976 Average}}$$

$$\text{\% Change} = \frac{\text{1976 Normalized Gap} - \text{1968 Normalized Gap}}{\text{1968 Normalized Gap}}$$

Example (median income):[9]

$$\text{1976 Normalized Gap} = \frac{(\$3428)}{\frac{\$11,645 + \$8217}{2}} = .345$$

$$\text{\% Change in normalized gap} = \frac{.345 - .461}{.461} = -25\%$$

---

8. Since 1968-1976 is an eight-year period as was 1960-1968, it is assumed for these calculations that the rates of change and, therefore, the proportion of change will remain the same for both periods.

9. The 1976 white and nonwhite levels, and the 1976 gap, are taken from the example above for Column 14.

Table 25. SUMMARY DATA TABLE

Columns 3–10 are on pages 68–71; columns 11–15, on pages 72–75

		DATA 1960	DATA 1968	Imputed annual rate of change 1960-1968[a]	Difference in imputed rates of change 1960-1968[b] (Rank)[c]
INDICATORS		1	2	3	4
LIVING CONDITIONS AND HEALTH					
Infant mortality (per 1000 population)[f]	W	17.2	14.7[g]	−2.0%	−0.2% (10)
	NW	26.9	23.4[g]	−1.8%	
Life expectancy at 35 years	W	73.8yr.	74.4yr.[g]	+0.10%	+0.02% (8)
	NW	69.3yr.	70.0yr.[g]	+0.12%	
HOUSING					
% Housing that is substandard	W	13%	6%	−9.2%	−1.9% (15)
	NW	44%	24%	−7.3%	
FAMILY					
% Female-headed families	W	8.7%	8.9%	+0.3%	−1.8% (14)
	NW	22.4%	26.4%	+2.1%	
% Children living with two parents	W	92%	92%	0.0%	−1.1% (12)
	NW	75%	69%	−1.1%	
Fertility rates (live births/1000 women, 15–44)	W	113	79.4[g]	−4.3%	−0.8% (11)
	NW	154	115.8[g]	−3.5%	
% Illegitimate births	W	2.3%	5.5%[g]	+11.4%	+6.9% (1)
	NW	21.6%	30.7%[g]	+4.5%	

a. The annual percentage change which would have given the 1960-1968 results if compounded annually from 1960 to 1968. All data in this table were rounded off after the calculations were performed.

b. A positive difference (+) means the rates tend toward decreasing the white/nonwhite differences.

c. For all rankings on this chart, the most favorable conditions (tending to reduce the gap) are ranked lowest (#1). The conditions indicating an increased gap are

SIZE AND CHANGE IN GAP

Size of white/ nonwhite gap, 1968	% Change in size of white/nonwhite gap 1960-1968 (Rank)[c]	Normalized gap—1968[d] (Rank)[c]	% Change in normalized gap 1960-1968[d] (Rank)[c]	Minimum required annual nonwhite rate resulting in a reduction of the gap size in 1969[e]	1960-1968 Nonwhite rate as a % of required rate (3) ÷ (9) (Rank)[c]
5	6	7	8	9	10
8.7	−11% (7-8)	.46 (6-7)	+3.5% (10)	−1.3%	143% (7)
4.4yr.	−2.2% (11)	.06 (1)	−3.9% (8)	+0.10%	117% (10)
18%	−42% (1)	1.2 (15)	+10% (12)	−2.3%	317% (2)
17.5%	+28% (14)	1.0 (13)	+13% (13)	+0.09%	h (16)
23%	+35% (16)	.29 (3)	+40% (16)	+0.0%	h (16)
36.4	−11% (7-8)	.37 (5)	+21% (14)	+3.0%	119% (9)
25.2%	+31% (15)	1.4 (16)	−14% (6)	+2.0%	h (16)

ranked highest (#16).

d. The gap size divided by the average level for whites and nonwhites for the year in question.
e. Assuming no change in white rate.
f. Infants dying before one month of age.
g. Computed data. 1968 value was computed using the 1960-1967 or 1960-1969 rates of change.
h. Most recent change is in the direction that will increase white/nonwhite differences.

(Continued on next page)

Table 25. **SUMMARY DATA TABLE** (continued)

Columns 3–10 are on pages 68–71; columns 11–15, on pages 72–75

		DATA		RATES OF CHANGE	
		1960	1968	Imputed annual rate of change 1960-1968[a]	Difference in imputed rates of change 1960-1968[b] (Rank)[c]
INDICATORS		1	2	3	4
EDUCATION					
% Men completing high school (25-29 years)	W B	63% 36%[h]	76% 58%	+2.3% +6.1%	+3.8% (5)
% Completing at least 4 years of college (25-34 years)	W B	11.7% 4.3%	15.7%[g] 6.3%[g]	+3.8% +4.9%	+1.1% (7)
EMPLOYMENT					
% Unemployed	W NW	4.9% 10.2%	3.2% 6.7%	−5.2% −5.1%	−0.1% (9)
% Teenagers unemployed	W NW	19.1% 34.2%	11%[g] 25%[g]	−6.7% −3.9%	−2.8% (16)
% In clerical occupations	W NW	15.8% 7.3%	17.5%[g] 12.1%[g]	+1.3% +6.6%	+5.3% (2)
% In professional and technical occupations	W NW	12.1% 4.8%	14.2%[g] 7.8%[g]	+2.0% +6.2%	+4.3% (4)
INCOME AND POVERTY					
Median family income (in 1968 dollars)	W NW	$6857 $3794	$8937 $5590	+3.4% +4.9%	+1.5% (6)
% Persons below poverty level	W B	18% 55%	10% 35%	−7.1% −5.5%	−1.6% (13)
% Families with incomes greater than $8,000 (in 1968 dollars)	W NW	39% 15%	58% 32%	+4.8% +10.0%	+5.2% (3)

a. The annual percentage change which would have given the 1960-1968 results if compounded annually from 1960 to 1968. All data in this table were rounded off after the calculations were performed.

b. A positive difference (+) means the rates tend toward decreasing the white/nonwhite differences.

c. For all rankings on this chart, the most favorable conditions (tending to reduce the gap) are ranked lowest (#1). The conditions indicating an increased gap are

SIZE AND CHANGE IN GAP

Size of white/nonwhite gap, 1968	% Change in size of white/nonwhite gap 1960-1968 (Rank)[c]	Normalized gap—1968[d] (Rank)[c]	% Change in normalized gap 1960-1968[d] (Rank)[c]	Minimum required annual nonwhite rate resulting in a reduction of the gap size in 1969[e]	1960-1968 Nonwhite rate as a % of required rate (3) ÷ (9) (Rank)[c]
5	6	7	8	9	10
18%	−33% (4)	.27 (2)	−51% (1-2)	+3.1%	193% (5)
9.0%	+21% (13)	.82 (12)	−12% (7)	+9.5%	51% (13)
3.5%	−34% (3)	.71 (10)	+.74% (9)	−2.5%	205% (4)
14%	−7.5% (10)	.78 (11)	+37% (15)	−2.9%	132% (8)
5.4%	−37% (2)	.36 (4)	−51% (1-2)	+1.8%	361% (1)
6.4%	−13% (6)	.58 (8-9)	−33% (4)	+3.6%	172% (6)
$3347	+9.3% (12)	.46 (6-7)	−20% (5)	+5.4%	90% (12)
25%	−32% (5)	1.1 (14)	+9.5% (11)	−2.0%	270% (3)
26%	+8.3% (9)	.58 (8-9)	−35% (3)	+8.7%	115% (11)

ranked highest (#16).
d. The gap size divided by the average level for whites and nonwhites for the year in question.
e. Assuming no change in white rate.
g. Computed data. 1968 value was computed using the 1960-1967 or 1960-1969 rates of change.
h. 1960 data are for nonwhites.

(Continued on next page)

Table 25. **SUMMARY DATA TABLE** (continued)

Columns 3–10 are on pages 68–71; columns 11–15, on pages 72–75

		DATA 1960	DATA 1968	Year nonwhites may reach 1968 white level (Rank)[c]	
		1	2	11	
LIVING CONDITIONS & HEALTH					
Infant mortality (per 1000 population)[f]	W NW	17.2 26.9	14.7[g] 23.4[g]	1994	(12)
Life expectancy at 35 years	W NW	73.8yr. 69.3yr.	74.4yr.[g] 70.0yr.[g]	2019	(13)
HOUSING					
% Housing that is substandard	W NW	13% 44%	6% 24%	1988	(9)
FAMILY					
% Female-headed families	W NW	8.7% 22.4%	8.9% 26.4%	never	(16)
% Children living with two parents	W NW	92% 75%	92% 69%	never	(16)
Fertility rates (live births/1000 women, 15-44)	W NW	113 154	79.4[g] 115.8[g]	1979	(6)
% Illegitimate births	W NW	2.3% 21.6%	5.5%[g] 30.7%[g]	never	(16)

c. For all rankings on this chart, the most favorable conditions (tending to reduce the gap) are ranked lowest (#1). The conditions indicating an increased gap are ranked highest (#16).

d. The gap size divided by the average level

ANALYSIS			IF NONWHITE AND WHITE RATES STAY THE SAME—1976 CONDITIONS					
Required annual nonwhite rate for nonwhites to reach 1968 white level by 1976	1960-1968 Nonwhite rate as a % of required rate (3) ÷ (12) (Rank)[c]		Possible % change in white/nonwhite gap size 1968-1976 (Rank)[c]		Possible % change in normalized gap 1968-1976[d] (Rank)[c]			
12	13		14		15			
−5.6%	32%	(12)	−11%	(10)	+3.5%	(10)		
+0.76%	16%	(13)	−3.4%	(11)	−3.1%	(7)		
−15.0%	48%	(8)	−43%	(3)	+8.3%	(12)		
−12.7%	h	(16)	+26%	(15)	+10%	(13)		
+3.8%	h	(16)	+24%	(14)	+28%	(16)		
−4.6%	76%	(6)	−14%	(9)	+17%	(14)		
−19.4%	h	(16)	+21%	(13)	−23%	(6)		

for whites and nonwhites for the year in question.
f. Infants dying before one month of age.
g. Computed data. 1968 value was computed using the 1960-1967 or 1960-1969 rates of change.
h. Most recent change is in the direction that will increase white/nonwhite differences.

73

Table 25. **SUMMARY DATA TABLE** (continued)

Columns 3–10 are on pages 68–71; columns 11–15, on pages 72–75

		DATA 1960	1968	Year nonwhites may reach 1968 white level (Rank)[c]
		1	2	11
EDUCATION				
% Men completing high school (25-29 years)	W B	63% 36%[h]	76% 58%	1973 (1)
% Completing at least 4 years of college (25-34 years)	W B	11.7% 4.3%	15.7%[g] 6.3%[g]	1987 (8)
EMPLOYMENT				
% Unemployed	W NW	4.9% 10.2%	3.2% 6.7%	1982 (7)
% Teenagers unemployed	W NW	19.1%[g] 34.2%[g]	11% 25%	1989 (10)
% In clerical occupations	W NW	15.8% 7.3%	17.5%[g] 12.1%[g]	1974 (2-3)
% In professional and technical occupations	W NW	12.1% 4.8%	14.2%[g] 7.8%[g]	1978 (4)
INCOME AND POVERTY				
Median family income (1968$)	W NW	$6857 $3794	$8937 $5590	1978 (5)
% Persons below poverty level	W B	18% 55%	10% 35%	1992 (11)
% Families with incomes greater than $8,000 (1968$)	W NW	39% 15%	58% 32%	1974 (2-3)

c. For all rankings on this chart, the most favorable conditions (tending to reduce the gap) are ranked lowest (#1). The conditions indicating an increased gap are ranked highest (#16).

d. The gap size divided by the average level

ANALYSIS			IF NONWHITE AND WHITE RATES STAY THE SAME—1976 CONDITIONS					
Required annual nonwhite rate for nonwhites to reach 1968 white level by 1976	1960-1968 Nonwhite rate as a % of required rate (3) ÷ (12) (Rank)[c]		Possible % change in white/nonwhite gap size 1968-1976 (Rank)[c]		Possible % change in normalized gap 1968-1976[d] (Rank)[c]			
12	13		14		15			
+3.5%	169%	(1)	−110%	(2)	−107%	(2)		
+12.2%	40%	(10)	+34%	(16)	−2.8%	(8)		
−9.0%	57%	(7)	−34%	(5)	+0.8%	(9)		
−9.4%	41%	(9)	−15%	(8)	+26%	(15)		
+4.7%	139%	(2)	−114%	(1)	−110%	(1)		
+7.9%	78%	(5)	−40%	(4)	−54%	(4)		
+6.0%	82%	(4)	+2.4%	(12)	−25%	(5)		
−14.5%	38%	(11)	−33%	(6)	+8.1%	(11)		
+7.6%	132%	(3)	−30%	(7)	−60%	(3)		

for whites and nonwhites for the year in question.

g. Computed data. 1968 value was computed using the 1960-1967 or 1960-1969 rates of change.

h. 1960 data are for nonwhites.

75

Table 26. **A RANKING ANALYSIS OF SELECTED DATA**[a]

	RATES OF CHANGE	CHANGES IN WHITE/NONWHITE GAP		
	Difference in imputed rates of change 1960-1968 (Rank)[c]	% Change in size of white/nonwhite gap, 1960-1968 (Rank)[d]	Possible % change in white/nonwhite gap size, 1960-1968 (Rank)[e]	1960-1968 Nonwhite rate as a % of required rate for reducing gap in 1969 (3) ÷ (9) (Rank)[f]
INDICATOR	4[b]	6	14	10
LIVING CONDITIONS AND HEALTH				
Infant mortality	10	7-8	10	7
Life expectancy	8	11	11	10
HOUSING				
% Housing substandard	15	1	3	2
FAMILY				
% Female-headed families	14	14	15	16
% Children with two parents	12	16	14	16
Fertility rates	11	7-8	9	9
% Illegitimate births	1	15	13	16
EDUCATION				
% Men completing high school	5	4	2	5
% Completing at least four years college	7	13	16	13
EMPLOYMENT				
% Unemployed	9	3	5	4
% Teenagers unemployed	16	10	8	8
% In clerical jobs	2	2	1	1
% In professional and technical occupations	4	6	4	6
INCOME AND POVERTY				
Median family income	6	12	12	12
% Persons below poverty level	13	5	6	3
% Income over $8000	3	9	7	11

a. Ranks are the same as those used in Table 25. The lowest number (1) indicates the least white/nonwhite difference.
b. Column numbers correspond to those used in Table 25.
c. Ranks 9-16 show a tendency for white/nonwhite differences to become larger.
d. Ranks 9-16 show the white/nonwhite gap increased.
e. Ranks 12-16 show the white/nonwhite gap may increase.
f. Ranks 12-16 show nonwhite rate is not

COMPOSITE MEASURES

Normalized gap—1968 (Rank)[g]	% Change in normalized gap, 1960-1968 (Rank)[h]	Possible change in normalized gap, 1968-1976 (Rank)[i]	Year nonwhites may reach 1968 white level (Rank)[j]	1960-1968 Nonwhite rate as a % of required rate to reach 1968 white level by 1976 (3) ÷ (12) (Rank)[k]
7	8	15	11	13
6-7	10	10	12	12
1	8	7	13	13
15	12	12	9	8
13	13	13	16	16
3	16	16	16	16
5	14	14	6	6
16	6	6	26	16
2	1-2	2	1	1
12	7	8	8	10
10	9	9	7	7
11	15	15	10	9
4	1-2	1	2-3	2
8-9	4	4	4	5
6-7	5	5	5	4
14	11	11	11	11
9	3	3	2-3	3

large enough to reduce the gap.

g. Ranks 13-16 show normalized gap is greater than 1.0.
h. Ranks 9-16 show normalized gap increased.
i. Ranks 10-16 show normalized gap may increase.
j. Ranks 1-3 show nonwhites may reach 1968 white levels before 1976.
k. Ranks 1-3 show that nonwhite rates are large enough to reach 1968 white level by 1976.

77

Appendix B

Methodology and Data Quality

Calculation of the Rate of Change

Only two data points were used to estimate a rate of change. Greater accuracy in establishing recent trends and their projections into the future could have been obtained through the use of extended time series (data for more years), but the methods available to do this would have been more subjective had graphic techniques been used, or more complex had computer curve fitting-techniques been used. The use of an imputed annual compound interest rate, which assumes an exponential growth curve, easily permits the mathematical projection of various interest rates by applying the compound interest formula. In future work it may be decided to use the average rate of change between the two points instead of the compound interest rate because of its common acceptance and ease of computation.

The technique of using only two points to calculate rates of change neglects to correct for the effects of the business cycle in many of the indicators, although this is offset somewhat by highlighting the different responses of white and nonwhite data to the same phases of the business cycle.

Measuring Changes in Percentage Figures

Because the data presentation is user-oriented, great effort was made to find some means of quantifying the changes in percentage figures over time. Since these percentages are often displayed in a manner which invites comparison—without any guides for interpreting the change—it was decided that subtracting percentages and calculating the percentage change between two different percentages, even though such calculations are not customary, was preferable to giving the reader no assistance in evaluating changing percentages.

A graphic presentation of changing percentages, while letting the reader visualize the changes, does not quantify the changes. Without some sort of quantification there would have been no way of comparing the changes in many different data series, as is done in Chapter 1.

The Quality of the Data

Most of the data for the intra-decennial census years (1967, 1968, 1969) were obtained from the approximately 50,000 households that are queried monthly by the Current Population Survey (CPS).[1] In order to insure compatibility with the CPS data, special tabulations were prepared from the 53,000 households in a one-in-a-thousand sample of the 1960 United States Census. As in any survey work, the results are subject to errors of response and of reporting, as well as subject to sampling variability.

Data for overall characteristics such as age, family structure, and education include inmates of institutions, but exclude all Armed Forces members living in barracks. The income, poverty, and employment data exclude both inmates of institutions and Armed Forces personnel living in barracks.

---

1. The description applies to the data used in the two sources which were used for the data included in this report, i.e., *The Social and Economic Status of Negroes in the United States, 1969,* and Current Population Reports, "Trends in Social and Economic Conditions in Metropolitan Areas."

The Urban Institute Board of Trustees

Arjay Miller, *Chairman*
Dean, Graduate School of Business
Stanford University
Stanford, Calif.

William W. Scranton, *Vice Chairman*
U. S. Ambassador
Scranton, Pa.

Ivan Allen, Jr.
Chairman, Ivan Allen Co.
Atlanta, Ga.

Roy L. Ash
President, Litton Industries, Inc.
Beverly Hills, Calif.

Jean Fairfax
Director, Division of Legal Information and Community Service
NAACP Legal Defense and Educational Fund, Inc.
New York, N.Y.

William C. Friday
President, University of North Carolina
Chapel Hill, N.C.

Eugene G. Fubini
Consultant
Arlington, Va.

John W. Gardner
Chairman, Common Cause
Washington, D.C.

William Gorham
President, The Urban Institute
Washington, D.C.

Katharine Graham
President, The Washington Post Co.
Washington, D.C.

Robert V. Hansberger
President, Boise Cascade Corporation
Boise, Idaho

William H. Hastie
Senior U. S. Circuit Court Judge
Philadelphia, Pa.

Edward Hirsch Levi
President, The University of Chicago
Chicago, Ill.

Bayless A. Manning
Professor, School of Law
Stanford University
Stanford, Calif.

Stanley Marcus
President, Neiman-Marcus
Dallas, Texas

Robert S. McNamara
President, International Bank for Reconstruction and Development
Washington, D.C.

J. Irwin Miller
Chairman, Cummins Engine Co., Inc.
Columbus, Ind.

Franklin D. Murphy
Chairman, The Times Mirror Co.
Los Angeles, Calif.

Charles L. Schultze
Senior Fellow, The Brookings Institution
Washington, D.C.

Franklin A. Thomas
President, Bedford-Stuyvesant Restoration Corp.
New York, N.Y.

Cyrus R. Vance
Partner, Simpson, Thacher & Bartlett
New York, N.Y.

James Vorenberg
Professor, School of Law
Harvard University
Cambridge, Mass.